A JOURNEY

THROUGHOUT IRELAND.

———

Vol. 1

Clachan Publishing,
Ballycastle : Northern Ireland,   2013

A Journey throughout Ireland, During the Spring, Summer and
Autumn of 1834, Vol. 2, Part 2,

Kerry, Clare, The Shannon, Limerick and Athlone

By Henry D. Inglis

Clachan Publishing
3 Drumavoley Park, Ballycastle, BT54 6PE,
County Antrim.
Email; info@clachanpublishing.com
Website: http://clachanpublishing-com.
ISBN - 978-1-291-36812-3

This edition published 2013

Original edition London:
Whittaker & Co., Ave-Maria Lane. 1835.
34 Farrington Street, London:

Clachan
Publishing

IRELAND IN 1834.

A

JOURNEY THROUGHOUT

IRELAND,

DURING THE

SPRING, SUMMER, AND AUTUMN OF
1834.

BY

HENRY D. INGLIS,

AUTHOR OF "SPAIN IN 1830," "THE CHANNEL ISLANDS,"
"THE TYROL," &c.

Second Edition.

IN TWO VOLUMES.

VOL 1.

Part 2.

LONDON:
WHITTAKER & CO., AVE-MARIA LANE.

1835.

Contents

CHAPTER I. - Cove, Cork, Blarney, Skibbereen, Bantry, Kenmare — 1

The Cove of Cork — Descent of the River Lee — Cove Town and Harbour — Means of improvement of Cove — Boating — Excursion to Blarney — Blarney Castle — " The Groves of Blarney" — The Kissing-stone — Journey to Bantry — Banilon — Clonakilty — Ross-Carherry — Picturesque Scenery — Proofs of Poverty — Skibbereen — Bantry, and its Bay — Cultivation of Bog Land — Coral Sand as Manure — Road to Glengariff — Scenery of Glengariff — Passage across the Mountains — Kenmare — Improving Condition of Kenmare — The surrounding Country, and Banks of the Kenmare River — The Barony of Glanrought, and Lord Lansdowne's Estates — Impressions, Facts, and Details — Land and Rents — Condition of the People — Blackwater Bridge — The New Road from Bantry to Kenmare.

CHAPTER II. - Killarney and its lakes — 16

The Town of Killarney — Idleness and Pauperism — Lord Kenmare — Bad Feeling among the Aristocracy, and its Causes — The Lakes — The Author's Opinion of Killarney Lakes — Their Character — Upper Lake, Turc Lake, Lower Lake — Glena — Innisfallen — The Echoes — Comparison with the English Lakes — Muckross Abbey — The Earl of Kenmare's Domain

CHAPTER III. - Kerry, Killorglin, Cahir-siveen, Valencia Island, Dingle — 23

Journey through the Wilds of Kerry — Castlemain Bay — Killorglin — Lord Headly's Estate — Sea Views — O'Connell's Country — The Agitator in his own Country — The Grand Jury Bill — An Anecdote — Cahir-siveen — Condition of the Landholders — Intelligence of the Kerry Peasantry — Examples — Valentia Island — Voyage across the Bay of Dingle — Dingle, and the Condition of the People — Peculiarities of the Inhabitants of this district — Extreme early Marriages — The Catholic Clergy,

and proposed Provision for them — Brandon Bay — The Tithe
Question — Journey to Tralee.

CHAPTER IV - Tralee, Listowel and Tarbert, Ennis   34

Tralee — The Quarter Sessions in Tralee — The Civil and Criminal
Cause List — State of Kerry-Faction — The Police of Ireland —
Litigiousness of the Irish — Prosperity of Tralee Trade — Prices of
Provisions — Unemployed Poor — Journey to Listowel and Tarbert
— Traits of Character — First View of the Shannon — Details —
Tarbert, and the Shores of the Shannon — Irish Inns of the West —
Steam Navigation on the Shannon — Ascent of the Shannon to
Limerick — Road to Ennis — Clare, and the River Fergus — Ennis
— Land, and High Rents — Environs of Ennis.

CHAPTER V. - Clare   49

Clare Assizes — English and Irish Assizes — Description of Cases
tried — Fair Murders — Spirit of Faction — Difficulty of eliciting
Truth — Disregard of an Oath — Extent to which Faction is carried
— A paid Magistracy necessary — Rape Cases — Abduction —
Murder — Assaults — Kissing the Book — Superstitions — General
Impressions from attending an Irish Assize

CHAPTER VI - Limerick, the Shannon, Adair   57

Return to Limerick — The New and Old Towns — Present State of
the Trade of Limerick — Prosperity — Projected Improvements —
Mr. Spring Rice — Public Institutions — The Lunatic Asylum — The
Barrington Hospital — Antiquities — Condition of the Destitute
Poor, and unemployed Artizans of Limerick — Minute Details —
Poor laws — a Mont de Pieti — Loan Fund — Environs of Limerick
— Lands and Rents — Embarkments on the Shannon — The Village
of Adair — Currah, and Dunraven

CHAPTER VII. The Shannon, Portumna,   68

Ascent of the Shannon, from Limerick to Athlone — Castle Connell
— The Rapids — Holy Well — The River above Castle Connell —
Killaloe — The Steam Navigation Company — Voyage up Loch
Derg to Portumna — Character of this expansion of the Shannon —
Details of the Ascent — Portumna — The River and its Banks
between Portumna and Banagber — Comparison with other Rivers
— Desolate Scenes — Banagher — Journey to Athlone.

CHAPTER VIII. Athlone   79

Henry D. Inglis

Henry David Inglis was born in Edinburgh in 1795 into an old Scottish family. Originally working in the world of business, he left this to develop careers as commentator, travel writer and newspaper editor. His initial experience of the world of business, however, equipped him with a keen awareness of the economic conditions and economic potential of the places he visited.

He also had a sensitive eye for the natural beauty of the countries he travelled through - and these included Norway, Sweden, Switzerland, France, and the Pyrenees, Tyrol and Spain. Nevertheless - the political social and economic condition of the peoples and their prospects was rarely far from his attention.

One of the major questions he asked as he set out on his tour of Ireland was 'is Ireland an improving Country?' and to answer this he examined agriculture, the role of the landlords, local and export trade, employment, wages and prices, among other things.

His trip took him through most of the counties in Ireland and many of its cities and towns. His observations provide a wealth of information on the social conditions he observed in each place. He observed poverty worse than he had seen in any other country and his analysis of many of Ireland's problems were well received at the time and informed much of the debate about Ireland in the Westminster House of Commons, during parliamentary debates in 1835.

This is an important historical document for all historians of Ireland, especially those interested in the social and economic conditions that prevailed after Catholic emancipation in the period after between the European Napoleonic Wars and the Great Famine. It is also an interesting insight into the religious attitudes and tensions which have divided Ireland over the centuries.

His observations reflect his own background, attitudes and beliefs which in themselves give us a additional insight into history. Nonetheless, they are grounded in specific details of the actual conditions he encountered first-hand. Its wealth of detail about the people he met, the towns and countryside he visited make it a very significant resource for genealogists and family and local historians.

Editor's Foreword

Clachan Publishing is a printing service dedicated to the preservation and promotion of print material related to Irish local and family histories. We produce books that are of local or family interest, such as memoires, articles, collections of old photographs, old letters, papers, newspaper cuttings, brochures, scrapbooks. We rely on materials given or lent to us by members of the public as well as commentaries and reports written by contemporaries of historic events.

The present publication, *A Journey throughout Ireland, During the Spring, Summer and Autumn of 1834*, Vol. 1, Part 2, by Henry D. Inglis, part of our series **'Local Histories'** series and is a continuation of Inglis' journey from through Ireland. His journey takes him through Killarney, the West of Kerry Tralee, Listowel, Counties Clare, Limerick and Athlone. His mission was to establish if Ireland was an 'improving county' and his observations give an insight into living standards and the relationship between the gentry, middlemen and the tenantry, as well as conditions in the towns he visited.

Being in the public domain, we are happy to reproduce this book in print form and extend its readership in accordance with our mission to promote historic material of interest to local and family historians.

The text has been edited to make it more accessible. Explanatory footnotes have been added. Older spellings and symbols have been modernized, paragraphing and punctuation are as in the original. We have added an index in order to help the reader navigate the text easily. Illustrations, except the map opposite, did not appear in the original text.

As this is a copy of an earlier publication, we cannot take responsibility for errors that may have occurred in the original. We wish to point out that the author's understandings reflect the views of his time, not present knowledge. We do, however, take responsibility for any errors that may have resulted from the formatting and printing processes.

We only claim copyright of this text in so far as it has been annotated and indexed. We request that anyone who uses materials from this publication acknowledge this as the source.

Seán O'Halloran, EDITOR, Clachan Publishing, Friday, March 29, 2013.

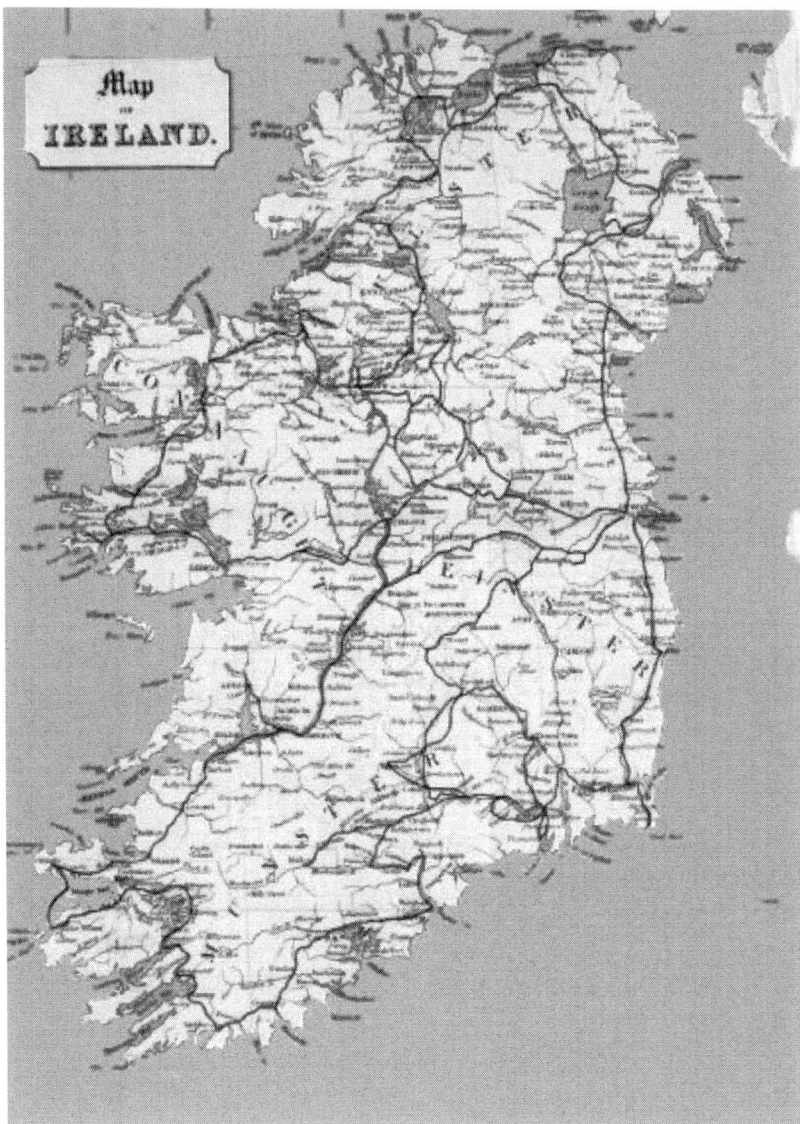

Map
OF
IRELAND.

TO
MATTHEW BARRINGTON, ESQ.

My Dear Sir,

It is not, believe me, in the foolish vanity of supposing I *confer* a favour, that I dedicate these volumes to you; nor is it even meant, in some sort, as an acknowledgment of the many aids and kindnesses for which I stand your debtor: that debt would continue undiminished, if I were to dedicate to you fifty books, — better than any I either have written, or ever shall write. I have better reasons than these, for my dedication.

Sitting over my coffee, devouring "The Last Days of Pompeii," this note was handed to me : —

"Sir, — We only wait for the contents, and dedication, in order to put the last sheet to press."

The dedication! Why, I never thought of a dedication: — " let the *devil* wait, — and shut the door."

No, said I, — laying down my pen, which I had hastily dipped in the ink, — and ringing the bell; I'll not do the thing in a hurry. There's no occasion to wait; I'll send the dedication tomorrow.

This, said I, — drawing my great chair in front of the fire, and placing my slippered feet on the fender, — this is not a thing which ought to be done hastily: a book need not, indeed, have a dedication at all; but, if there be a dedication, it ought to be a judicious one.

   *   *   *   *   *   *   *   *   *   *

My book, said I, musingly, and gently tapping the fire, — is a truth-telling book, — it is no party book, — and, God knows — (while a thousand images of appalling misery, and hopeless poverty, — not poetical fancies, but stern realities — thronged upon my memory), — God knows I feel acutely for the people of this unhappy land. I will dedicate my book to some one, who knows thoroughly, the country and its needs; some one who is no hot and headstrong partizan: some one, who has the good of his country at heart, and who has proved it too.

I wheeled my chair round, and wrote this dedication; and I do most solemnly aver, that if I knew any man better acquainted with Ireland and her people than yourself, — if I knew a man who holds in greater detestation, the extremes of party, — if I knew a man who loves his country better, or would serve it more faithfully than you, — or one who has given more disinterested proofs of sympathy with the helpless poor, — I would dedicate my book to that man. But I know of no such man.

On some points of minor importance, our opinions may not, perhaps, entirely coincide. In the main, however, I trust, we are agreed: and when I say, that the people of Ireland are oppressed by some, deluded by others, and neglected by all — and that, notwithstanding the folly, and knavery, and neglect, with which Ireland has been, and is, cursed — she needs but a seed-time of kind deeds, in order that a harvest of abundant blessings may be reaped, I anticipate a cordial — *Amen.*

Hoping that your days, like those of your respected father, Sir Joseph, may be prolonged, — and that you may, after long years of kind deeds and usefulness, crown "a life of labour with an age of ease" and honour,

I remain,

My dear Sir,

Yours, most faithfully,

HENRY D. INGLIS.

London, November 1834.

A JOURNEY

THROUGHOUT IRELAND.

CHAPTER I.

Cove, Cork, Blarney, Skibbereen, Bantry, Kenmare

The Cove of Cork — Descent of the River Lee — Cove Town and Harbour — Means of improvement of Cove — Boating — Excursion to Blarney — Blarney Castle — " The Groves of Blarney" — The Kissing-stone — Journey to Bantry — Banilon — Clonakilty — Ross-Carberry — Picturesque Scenery — Proofs of Poverty — Skibbereen — Bantry, and its Bay — Cultivation of Bog Land — Coral Sand as Manure — Road to Glengariff — Scenery of Glengariff — Passage across the Mountains — Kenmare — Improving Condition of Kenmare — The surrounding Country, and Banks of the Kenmare River — The Barony of Glanrought, and Lord Lansdowne's Estates — Impressions, Facts, and Details — Land and Rents — Condition of the People — Blackwater Bridge — The New Road from Bantry to Kenmare.

Everybody has heard of the Cove of Cork. From the city to Cove, it is about nine miles by the nearest road; and by water, it is eleven. In my journey from Youghall to Cork, I had seen just enough of the banks of the Lee, to give me the desire to see more of them; and I therefore took advantage of the steam vessel, which leaves Cork for Cove every morning. "Have you been to Cove?" "Have you seen the banks of our river?" are questions often and eagerly put to the stranger in Cork; and well may the question be put: for it is quite certain that if the stranger has visited Cove, he will reply,

$\overline{1}$

"Yes, I have; and I have seldom seen any thing more beautiful." The broad river — in reality an arm of the sea, but which has all the appearance of a lake — stretches below the city in a magnificent reach of five or six miles; high swelling banks rise on both sides; and these, the whole way to Passage, exhibit the most charming succession of lawns, woods, and pleasure grounds, appertaining to the numerous villas that embellish them: and these are indeed villas, or something beyond villas; not boxes with their acre, or half-acre of lawn, shrubbery, and garden; but handsome houses, with room enough about them, to give them an air of independence and respectability. Between Cork and Passage, I counted upwards of thirty such houses, calculated, I should say, for the residence of persons with from £1500 to £3000 a year. Besides these, there are innumerable citizens' boxes nearer to the city; and especially, on the banks of the river higher up; many of them worthy the name of villa, and all, pretty snug places.

Two villages are passed on the right bank of the river, between Cork and Cove. Black Rock is the first of these; and it is only remarkable for the extensive nunnery, which stands facing the river. Passage is lower down; and is beautifully situated, just where the wide reach of the river ends, and where it contracts into little more than river width. Beyond this narrow reach, the river sweeps to the left, and discovers at a little distance, the magnificent Cove with its islands and town.

The Cove of Cork means, in England, a large sea basin, situated near to Cork: but the Cork people call the Cove, the harbour; and by *Cove,* they mean the town which is built there; while many of us at home, scarcely know that there is such a town as Cove. But Cove is not only a town; but a considerable town, and a pretty town; and the most fashionable sea-bathing place in the south of Ireland.

Cove town is situated on the side of the great basin, and on a considerable eminence, and commands a magnificent view over *the* Cove, with its islands, and rich shores; and — beyond Spike Island — the narrow entrance from the Atlantic, and the ocean beyond it. It chanced to be within a week or two of the regatta when I visited Cove; and ten or twelve of the yachts were sweeping to and fro, with full sail, under the influence of a fine light breeze. Yachting and boating are quite a passion in this neighbourhood; and although this, like another passion I have named, tends in some degree, to encourage the disposition towards improvidence, which is so truly a characteristic of the Irish nation — yet the public benefit by it. Yachting gives employment to many; and the frequent meetings of the club contribute greatly to the prosperity of Cove; which, however, is far from being so prosperous, as from the many advantages it possesses, it might be expected to be.

Nothing is wanting to render Cove a most flourishing town, but the outlay of some thousand pounds on the erection of houses for the accommodation of strangers. At present, houses and lodgings are very scarce and very dear. I inquired the rent of a small furnished house — a mere box, with a few square yards of garden, and found it to be £20 a month. For another — a house of two stories — each story with four windows in front, I was asked a hundred guineas for three months. From these prices, it is evident that there is no supply equal to the demand; and that £10,000 judiciously laid out, would be very advantageously invested. But nothing is done for the town in this way. Mr. Smith Barry, who is a good resident landlord, and a public spirited man, is prevented I believe by certain circumstances, from granting leases; and the other great proprietor, Lord Middleton, an absentee, either knows nothing, or cares nothing about Cove and its wants. These are misfortunes for Cove: for situated as it is, in so beautiful a country; so near to Cork; with a fashionable reputation, and with extraordinary advantages of climate, much might be made of Cove. I was happy to learn that a literary society and library, had lately been established at Cove; and that the institution was flourishing. I ought to have mentioned, when speaking of boating, that Cove and Cork men, row in a peculiar manner. -They make a double dip: after immersing the oar, they make a half pull, and then dip, and pull again. This mode of rowing is not elegant, though it is said to be effective.

Who would be at Cork without visiting Blarney, which is situated about six miles from Cork? The road to it lies up the bank of the Lee, and conducts the traveller through a succession of very pretty scenes. The Castle stands upon an eminence, and consists of one very massive square tower. There are many things more picturesque than Blarney Castle; but then, it is Blarney; and is therefore necessary to be visited; and there you'll see

> "The groves of Blarney, that are so charming[1]" —
> and the castle,
> "That was once so ancient" —
> and Blarney loch,
> "That holds its own sweet waters,
> That have rested in it since before the flood."

But Blarney loch, holds more than its own sweet waters; for it holds the most beautiful of white water-lilies, that fringe its margin, encircled by the great heart-shaped leaves that almost cover the surface. The Blarney-stone which every one is expected to kiss; and which embrace, confers on the kisser the power of flattering as much as he pleases, and of commanding the belief of those who are flattered, is on the top of the tower, and quite accessible to all who desire to profit by the opportunity.

From Cork to Bantry there are two roads: one of these is much shorter than the other; but I preferred the longer road, which passes through several considerable towns — Bandon, Clonakilty, Ross-Carberry, and Skibbereen. This is the road travelled by the mail; and by the mail I travelled. It is not a country possessing great interest; and I therefore contented myself with passing through it. Mail travelling in Ireland is not remarkable for its speed, or precise regulations: it ranks, I think, with the English slowest coaches; but it is a very safe mode of conveyance, for the drivers are extremely cautious; and it is also cheap. In speed, regularity, and even cheapness, Bianconi's cars leave the mails far behind.

The fine country, and good husbandry in the neighbourhood of Cork do not extend far in this direction. At the distance of but a few miles I found the land under very imperfect cultivation; and all

---

[1] Amused by the absurdity of the popular song *Castle Hyde*, Richard Alfred Millikin declared he would write a piece even more absurd. With this view he wrote the popular *Groves of Blarney*, [Clachan ed.].

of it, susceptible of great improvement. Near to Bandon, the appearance of the country improves; and there is a slight approach to the picturesque, in following the course of the river. Bandon was once a flourishing manufacturing town; but its manufactures have some time ceased: and although the immediate destitution occasioned by the loss of trade, has been somewhat cured by emigration and otherwise, Bandon is at present a poor town, and is stocked with paupers. I did not stop to make any particular inquiries; and can therefore speak of Bandon only as I saw it, *en passant.*

From Bandon, the road winds through a bare, ill-cultivated country, to Clonakilty. Proceeding in this direction, things appeared to be evidently getting worse. The cabins almost reminded me of Callen; and every thing had a poor, neglected aspect. Clonakilty is another decayed town: — there was formerly a good linen trade in it; but that manufacture does not now exist; and the town is at present without any means of support, except that which arises from agricultural labour, and the more precarious trade of fishing. I noticed much obvious misery; and the number of bare-footed persons had greatly increased. The effect produced on the traveller by the spectacle of bare feet and legs, depends very much on the state of the weather, and upon other circumstances. A healthy looking girl, tripping along a country road, or field path, without shoes or stockings, suggests no want of comfort; but to see the streets of a town, on a rainy day, trodden by multitudes of bare feet — many the feet of old persons — creates a very different impression, and the impression is a just one. It is impossible to believe that any one would walk bare-footed, on wet, ill-paved streets, from choice; but I know it to be often matter of choice in the country. I have seen a gentleman — a man of family and fortune, and a magistrate — walking through the fields, carrying his boots in his hands, for greater coolness and freedom.

After leaving Clonakilty, the country, although not any better cultivated, becomes more agreeable; and the approach to Ross-Carberry, is extremely picturesque. It stands on an elevation, at the head of a long narrow inlet of the sea, flanked by wooded banks, and itself half hidden in wood. We skirted the town; and stopped just opposite to the Courthouse, where a petty sessions had been held. The court had just broken up; and the room emptied itself of as ragged a population as I had yet any where seen. I scarcely saw one woman or girl with shoes or stockings; and here, for the first time, I observed a considerable number of the men also bare-footed. The Court-house is certainly not the place where any one would have gone barefooted from choice.

After leaving this town, the country became extremely picturesque. We passed along, and round the heads of deep, winding, wooded inlets of the sea, — reminding me, in some degree, of Norwegian scenery on a small scale; and soon after reached Skibbereen, a small ugly town; but a busy and thriving town; enjoying an excellent retail trade, owing to the demand of an extensive surrounding district.

It is a very poor and uninteresting country that lies between Skibbereen and Bantry; the greater part of it is bog land: some small part of it indeed reclaimed; but a large portion which human labour has never approached. On some parts, where little pools of water had collected, the water-lilies, white and yellow, were numerous; and on others, the beautiful white tufts of the bog-cotton, relieved the dreariness of the prospect. The approach to Bantry is pretty. Rounding a little inlet, one suddenly reaches the margin of the bay; and, keeping its waters on the left, and the domain of Lord Bantry on the right, ten minutes more brings one into the little town, and to the very indifferent inn, or hotel, as I believe it is called, which the town affords.

Bantry lies at the head of the celebrated bay which bears its name; encircled by hills, or at least by considerable elevations, many of which are tolerably cultivated, and wooded. Lord Bantry is the great proprietor here, and is universally well spoken of. His lordship is for the most part resident; and as far as his means will permit, he consults the benefit of the town, and the comfort of the people. Much might be done for Bantry, as a sea-bathing resort; and money judiciously laid out, would certainly be invested to advantage. There was formerly a considerable fishery at Bantry; but it has now failed — the fish having changed their place of resort.

For the cultivation of the bog land in this neighbourhood, extraordinary facilities are afforded; and owing to these, the country appears to be in a very improving condition. I allude particularly to the Bantry sea-sand; which is called there, coral sand, and which is allowed, by universal consent, to be the most efficacious of manures, for the improvement of every description of land, as well as for the reclamation of bog land. Common sea-sand is a very common manure, in many parts of this country; but the superior excellence of the Bantry coral sand is universally admitted, and is owing to the large proportion of lime which it contains.

My course now lay by Glengariff, Kenmare, and Killarney, to Tralee and the lower Shannon. The weather not permitting boating, I hired a car to carry me to Glengariff; and I question whether much was lost by the substitution of a land journey. The road winds round heights, and through hollows, generally wooded; and doubles a number of inlets of the sea; some of them open to the ocean; others having the appearance of lakes; and fine views are every now and then caught over Bantry Bay and its mountain boundaries.

Few spots offer a more perfect example of the picturesque, than Glengariff inn. It is situated at the head of a narrow creek, which runs up from the bay. High mountains form one of the boundaries of the creek; and the beautiful domain of Captain White, Lord Bantry's brother, forms the other. Rocks, rushing streams, wooded ravines, quiet coves, and a fine back-ground of mountains, are the elements of the landscape. I was not disappointed in Glengariff, because I had put little faith in the exaggerated reports I had heard and read. Visit Glengariff with the expectation of finding much that is picturesque, and you will not be disappointed; but if sublimity and the magnificence of nature be looked for, they will certainly not be found.

I visited, and was greatly pleased with Captain White's domain: it contains many beautiful spots; commands many fine mountain views; and is adorned by a fancifully built, but judiciously placed mansion. I found no complaint of want of work in this neighbourhood: the new road now in course of being formed, between Glengariff and Kenmare, employs several hundred hands; and the people upon Captain White's property, are generally comfortable. Few have less land than suffices for the keep of two cows, the rent of which is taken out in labour, at eight-pence a day. I dined sumptuously at Glengariff, on pink coloured, — there called, white trout, — caught an hour before; a dish of scalloped cockles, new potatoes, and flour scones: which, with a glass of parliament whiskey, helped to prepare me for the fatigue of the journey to Kenmare.

Most people travel this road on horseback; but not being able to get horse or pony to my mind, I hired a car, and two men to assist. These cannot well be dispensed with, unless the horse drag kindly up, and back well down hill. The road, though excessively bad, and so extremely steep that one must walk nearly the whole of the way, presents so many fine mountain views, that no one has any right to grumble. The rock scenery is particularly interesting; and, mixed with the oak and holly woods, above which the great rocks lift their broad backs, is not only of a picturesque, but of a very novel character. I left the road, to visit a lodge of Lord Bantry's, remarkable only for its seclusion, and for the clearness of the stream which rushes by; and took the opportunity of also visiting two houses, — in one of which I found a peasant who owned three acres, for which he paid £3; and in another, a peasant who owned three acres and a half, for which he paid £3 10s. It is a good mode of confirming the truth of what one hears from different individuals, to inquire not only as to their own circumstances, but also into those of their neighbours; if the statements of their neighbours correspond with their own, there is every reason to believe them correct.

I found the road as bad, but not so steep, as it had been represented. I believe the horse could have dragged up the car without assistance; but the men assured me, that in descending, I should find their aid indispensable. Just as we reached the summit of the pass, the mists, which had been floating about the mountains, — veiling the extent of the views, but adding perhaps to their beauty, — dispersed; the sun came brilliantly forth; and the whole of the mountains stood clearly out, with all their glens and shadows, and little silvery lakes. The descent I found to be indeed very rapid: the men had brought ropes, with which they endeavoured to lock the wheel, by attaching it to the axle; but the rope was rotten, and broke; and the descent was not accomplished without some scrambling.

From the foot of the mountain to Kenmare, I passed through an evidently improving country: the road was tolerably good: I saw several comfortable looking houses; and a greater number of lime kilns, the beneficial effects of which were evident in the appearance of the neighbouring land. Every farm, indeed, appeared to have a lime kiln of its own. A few miles before reaching Kenmare, the valley of the Kenmare river, and the river itself, are descried from a height over which the road passes. Soon after a bridge is crossed; and the road, running parallel with the river, and under a fine arch of trees, reaches the town.

Kenmare is a small, but very prettily situated town. The estuary, called the Kenmare river, reaches some miles above it; and from Kenmare to the sea, the distance is about twenty-six miles. The estuary varies in breadth, from two or three hundred yards, to upwards of a mile; and presents, in its whole line, the aspect of a magnificent river. I was struck by observing from the windows of the inn, what is rather a novel spectacle in the small Irish towns, — several large houses in course of building; and, upon walking over the town, I counted no fewer than eleven good houses in a state of forwardness: a considerable number of others seemed to be newly built; and although I observed six or eight houses in a ruined condition, I thought myself warranted in concluding, from what I had seen, that these were intended to be replaced by a better description of buildings. This I afterwards found, was to be immediately done. Extending my walk a little way out of the town, towards the river, I reached a new pier, from which, I was glad to learn, that corn had been shipped, for the first time, last autumn, for the English market. This neat little pier cost £2100, of which the Marquis of Lansdowne contributed £1200.

I spent two days in and about Kenmare, — one, of them, a long summer's day, mounted on a Kerry pony, riding down the opposite side of the Kenmare river, — riding and walking in and out among the mountain glens, and traversing the greater part of the Barony of Glanrought. I had a double enjoyment in the ramble: arising both from the charming weather and fine mountain views, and from the spectacle of a rapidly improving country, and a comparatively comfortable population.

I think I said, in a former chapter, that from the moment of setting foot in Ireland, I had heard the highest character of the property of the Duke of Devonshire; and that, on that account, I felt a more than usual interest in reaching Lismore. A precisely opposite reason increased the interest of a visit to Kenmare; for I had heard very indifferent accounts of the property of Lord Lansdowne; and was told in Cork, that I should find a miserable population, who were accustomed to shut up their cabins, and go a-begging for months during the summer. Now, it affords me the greatest pleasure to be able, from minute personal observation and inquiry, to bear testimony to the improving condition of this extensive and naturally barren tract, and to the comparatively comfortable condition of the people. Formerly, the greater part of this property was held in large farms, by lessees, who sub-let these lands in small portions, and therefore became middle-men. As these leases have dropped, by death, or otherwise, the estates, so held, have been divided into farms of equal size, and let to tenants holding immediately under Lord Lansdowne, who has erected upon each farm, a comfortable dwelling-house, the whole expense of which, excepting labour, has been defrayed by his lordship. Riding through this part of Kerry, one is immediately struck by the absence of mud cabins, and, by the presence of these new farm-like houses, everywhere dotting the slopes. Such things being rarities, I did not content myself with a distant view; but visited ten or twelve of these houses, and they seemed to me well suited to the wants of the individuals by whom they were occupied. There was nothing of pretension about them. I found them to be built of lime-water, rough-cast, with chimneys, and with two apartments inside; and generally containing a sufficiency of furniture, and a fair portion of comfort, — speaking always, let it be recollected, with reference to the character and habits of the people. And, what is most important of all, I did not find that the tenants were paying exorbitant rents. One tenant, occupying a little farm of nine acres, with one of these houses, paid £2 13s. for his possession; that is, about six shillings an acre. From one to two acres of this farm were under tillage; and the rest was in pasture, on which two cows were fed. I found another tenant occupying eighteen acres, paying for his farm £7 2s., or eight shillings an acre. This was somewhat more improved land; it supported four cows; and grew potatoes, corn, and flax. I found another, with thirty acres, paying £6 4s., or four shillings an acre. This was poorer land; but the farm supported six cows — though four would have been a more proper number — and grew a little wheat on low spots, and excellent potatoes. All of these farms had houses attached; and I certainly feel myself bound to say, from a very minute observation of these houses and lands, that these, and all the other tenants similarly circumstanced, held their land on terms, on which any industrious man might pay his rent, and support his family in that degree of comfort consistent with Irish notions.

There are other advantages too, which these tenants possess. Every one has turf, *a discretion,* for the trouble of cutting and fetching it; and as the whole of these lands lie along the Kenmare river, fish is easily attainable. I counted upwards of forty boats lying on the beach; and to the smaller tenants, whose farms are chiefly in pasture, and require little labour, the privilege of fishing is a most valuable one, both for the purposes of sale and subsistence.

During this day's ride, I counted fifty-seven farm-houses of the description I have mentioned; and I was informed, by the farmers, that I had not seen a third part of the number. Throughout the whole of this tract, there are not any of those mud cabins, with a small patch of potato land, which are so numerous in most parts of Ireland. No tenant holds a less quantity of land than about eight acres. I speak, at present, of land held immediately under Lord Lansdowne; for nothing will strike a traveller, in this country, more than the difference in the condition of land so held, and of that land which is held under several middle-men. I passed through some clusters of as miserable cabins as I ever beheld — twelve or fifteen of them congregated together. I went into several of these, and found that they were all held under lessee middle-men — some of them resident, and some absent. These cabins had but a small portion of land annexed, and were, beyond description, wretched abodes; and the inmates of two of them, told me, that they were in the habit of shutting up their cabins, and going, for a month or two, during autumn, in search of work, or livelihood, into Cork county, or elsewhere. If I had merely inquired upon whose estate these people lived, and heard from them that the estate was Lord Lansdowne's, without inquiring whether there was any intermediate holder, I should have thought I had found confirmation of the necessitous condition, and begging propensities, of that noble Lord's tenantry. It is proper for me to state, that I found several larger middle-men, excellent men, and improving landlords, and with no tenantry in the condition I have mentioned.

In the course of a ramble, up one of the distant glens, I fell in with two men holding mountain farms. These, as they, themselves, told me, had been holders of little more than cabins, under middle-men; and, when the lease expired, and the land was divided and appropriated among the existing tenants, these two, being considered to have least claim, and the original farm not being large enough to be divided among all those who had holdings on it, were turned upon mountain land: eight acres were given to one of the two, and fifteen to the other. One paid a rent of 2s. 6d. for his farm; the other 4s. They told me they could scarcely live out of their land; but I suspect industry was wanting, for on land close to theirs, I saw good corn and potatoes growing; and both lime and sea-sand are plentiful over this country. Idleness will make a pauper of any one; and it is impossible for any landlord altogether to exclude pauperism. Standing with a farmer, at the door of his house, I observed, in a hollow at a little distance, five or six - cottages in a ruined condition; but smoke issued from the door, and through holes in the roof of one of them. These, the farmer told me, were the cabins of those who had been on a farm, of which the lease had expired, and which was now divided; but he knew nothing of the inmate of the smoking cabin. I walked down to the hollow, and found a man, his wife, and three children, living in this roofless and utterly unfurnished hovel; and although, at first, I could get no other information than that they were tenants of Lord Lansdowne's, I ascertained, at length, that they had been tenants, of this same cabin, under a middle-man; and when the lease dropped, and the farm was divided, this individual was offered a mountain farm, which he would not accept; and, after having been wandering through different parts of the country, begging, he had returned, with his family, and taken possession of the cabin in which he had formerly lived.

I have dwelt the longer on the events of this day's ride, and on the condition of the property on the Kenmare river, because of the very unfavourable reports I had heard: and finding as I did, that these reports were utterly without foundation; and that this very untractable district, — so unfavourable in many respects to improvement, — exhibited those unerring signs of it, which can result only from a considerate landlord, and an intelligent agent, I felt it to be my duty to state the facts upon which I have grounded my opinion: and I would only add, that the more distant I was from these estates, the more unfavourable were the reports I heard of them; and in their immediate vicinity, and amongst those best qualified to judge, I heard nothing but the most favourable reports. I would take the liberty of particularly mentioning the Earl of Kenmare, — by universal consent, one of the best of landlords, — who spoke to me in the highest terms of the condition of the property to which I have so particularly alluded.

There is still one other observation I have to make, before proceeding on my journey. When we speak of a poor or a rich tenantry, we ought to speak with reference to the nature of the land. A rich population is not to be expected on a mountainous district, like the barony of Glanrought; and when we find tenants of mountain farms circumstanced as they are in this country, we ought to expect nothing beyond a very moderate share of comfort. Suppose a farm of a hundred acres to have been held by a middleman, and that thirty tenants are located upon it; this lease drops, and the landlord proceeds to divide. To continue these thirty tenants upon the hundred acres, giving little more than three acres to each, would only be, to perpetuate pauperism. The landlord has perhaps laid down a rule, that he will have no tenant with a smaller possession than eight acres; because, in an upland country, no man can be comfortable on a less quantity of land: the twelve most improving of the thirty tenants are therefore selected for holdings, each of eight acres, on these hundred acres; and the remaining eighteen become possessors of mountain holdings — not so good, indeed, as those possessed by the selected twelve; but vastly better to an industrious man, than no holding at all: and thus it will be seen, that poor, though not pauper tenants, must exist upon every improving estate, situated in an upland country.

Before leaving Kenmare I visited Blackwater bridge, which lies amongst the mountains, about six miles distant. It is a very agreeable ride to this spot, and the scene itself is beautiful. The river tumbles through a deep channel, in a ravine finely fringed by oak and ash trees; a high and very picturesque bridge of two arches spans the river; and I had there an opportunity of seeing the spectacle so often described, of the unwearied efforts of the fishes to get above the fall.

Kenmare, and all this district, will receive incalculable benefits from the fine road now constructing from Bantry to Cork: this road, which takes Glengariff in its line, will connect Killarney with Cork by a most interesting route; and it is intended to throw a bridge over the Kenmare river, or sound, as it is there called, just below the town.

I now left Kenmare, for Killarney. The first part of this excellent road is not particularly interesting. It leads through an upland, bare, and partly cultivated country, in which, however, there are signs of improvement, and some tolerably good houses; and after passing a lake and a few cottages, the descent towards Killarney begins. The first view one obtains of the upper lake of Killarney, is not striking: it disappointed me; but the weather was rather unfavourable for the enjoyment of scenery, and I suspended my judgment, although I could not alter the impression. The descent along the sides of the hills, and through the fine woods with which they are clothed, pleased me much; and here, for the first time, I saw, almost in its perfection, the arbutus — the far-famed pride of Killarney. I noticed here also, for the first time, that pretty little flower which forms sometimes our garden borders; and which is called, "London-pride," or " none-so-pretty." In descending to the lake, the road passes through a tunnel, which has a good effect, but which was certainly unnecessary; as a little more free use of gunpowder, would have entirely opened up the passage. Soon after passing through this tunnel, the road descends close to the shore of the upper lake, and winds first along part of its margin, and then continues to skirt a part of Turc lake, with the fine wooded elevation called Turc mountain, on the other side. There, however, the road leaves the lakes; and passing through a fine rich country, and skirting several domains, leads into the town.

CHAPTER II.

Killarney and its lakes

The Town of Killarney — Idleness and Pauperism —Lord Kenmare — Bad Feeling among the Aristocracy, and its Causes — The Lakes — The Author's Opinion of Killarney Lakes — Their Character — Upper Lake, Turc Lake, Lower Lake — Glena — Innisfallen — The Echoes — Comparison with the English Lakes — Muckross Abbey — The Earl of Kenmare's Domain.

Killarney suggests to an Englishman, merely a spot where lakes are situated: it is nothing but a name. But to one residing in the neighbourhood, it suggests a biggish, populous, noisy, and not very pretty town. The situation of the town is good, without being at all picturesque; for although, with a fine country around, it lies at least a mile and a half from the nearest point of the lakes. There are two good streets in the town; but many bad alleys, and close filthy lanes and yards; and I regret to say, that there is a large pauper population, and a vast number of idle persons, — some from necessity, and some from choice: for besides its own natural proportion of destitute and unemployed persons, Killarney has in addition, that class of the idly disposed and poor, who are either attracted to every spot much resorted to by strangers, or who are created, by the charm which precarious employment possesses in the estimation of many, over the more certain, but more moderate wages of labour.

Killarney is the property of the Earl of Kenmare; but his lordship is just as little answerable for the faults of Killarney, as the reader of this book. The whole of the town is held under leases for ever; so that Lord Kenmare has no power of improvement in his hands: and this is greatly to be regretted: for a better man, or a better landlord than Lord Kenmare, does not exist; and were it not for the employment afforded on his estate, by this wealthy resident and public spirited nobleman, the pauperism of Killarney would be fearfully great. A considerable part of Lord Kenmare's large estate, is in the hands of middle-men; but his lordship is strenuously exerting himself, to bring about a better system.

There is much bad feeling among the aristocracy in the neighbourhood of Killarney: and Lord Kenmare is far from being so popular among a 'certain class, as he deserves to be. Amongst the neighbouring gentry, there are many large middlemen, who are not fond of Lord Kenmare's reforming system; and there are also some of Mr. O'Connell's friends, and even some branches of his family, who cannot forgive the sin committed by the head of the Irish Catholic aristocracy, in being an anti-repealer, and a respecter of order; nor pardon the slight put upon them by Lord Kenmare, in selecting as his deputy lieutenants, men upon whom he thought he could depend for support, in time of emergency. Through these causes, bad feeling has been also excited among the lower classes, which is greatly to be regretted; because Lord Kenmare's religious opinions, and his high rank (for the Irish peasant has much respect for blood) might have otherwise exerted a most powerful influence on his numerous tenantry and dependents, — an influence which would certainly have been well exerted.

But I must not forget that there are such things as the lakes of Killarney; and although I have no intention of writing a guide to the lakes, I must not pass over with too slight a notice, objects deserving all the reputation they have acquired. To obtain any correct notion of the beauty of the Killarney lakes, it is necessary to embark at the head of the upper lake, and to descend the chain — a distance of about fifteen miles. The best way of accomplishing this, which may be accomplished in one day, is, to go from the town round the lower part of the lower lake, and by the gap of Dunlow. By this route one passes some fine seats — particularly that of Lord Headly, — and another, the residence of one of the O'Connell family. The mountain views, too, are fine, — particularly the views of McGillicuddy's reeks, and of another mountain, Carran Tual, which is now admitted to be the highest of the Irish mountains. This claim always carries some little interest with it; and Mangerton — always an ugly mountain, — divested as it now is, of its claim to being the highest, has become almost insignificant. The height of Mangerton, is 2550 feet; while that of Carran Tual, is 3410.

The gap of Dunlow did not seem to me, to be worthy of its reputation: it is merely a deep valley: but the rocks which flank the valley, are neither very lofty, nor very remarkable in their form; and although, therefore, the gap presents many features of the picturesque, its approaches to sublimity are very distant. I was more struck by the view after passing the gap, up what is called "the dark valley," — a wide and desolate hollow, surmounted by the finest peaks of this mountain range.

After passing the gap of Dunlow, and descending the steeps on the south side, I embarked at the head of the upper lake, and descended the chain of lakes, through many varied and most enchanting scenes. I saw Killarney to every advantage; for I was favoured by one of those warm days of sunshine and shade, which are particularly calculated for the enjoyment of mountain and lake scenery, — a sky, warm enough to give richness to the landscape; and yet, without the haziness which accompanies heat; and air, just enough to vary the effects of light and shade, on lake and mountain, without disturbing that tranquility which is the peculiar charm of lake scenery. I had likewise the advantage of Lord Kenmare's boat and rowers, and of the particular instructions which they had received from his lordship. If the traveller visit Killarney without those exaggerated notions which are apt to be conveyed by a guide book, he will certainly be satisfied and delighted. There is nothing of the sublime about Killarney; but there is all of that kind of beauty, which depends upon the combinations of form and colour. The mountain outlines can scarcely be finer than they are; and in the variety of colour produced by the variety of foliage, — from the beautiful bright green of the arbutus, to the brown mountain heath, — Killarney is eminently distinguished.

To my mind, the upper lake is the most attractive: the mountains are nearest to it; it has not one tame feature; and it is more studded with islands, than either of the other lakes. I landed upon several of the islands, and was delighted with the luxuriant vegetation; and above all, with the arbutus, which is here a great tree; and whose fresh tints, contrast so well with the grey rocks among which it grows. There is a sweet secluded cottage on the shore of this lake, usually called Hyde's cottage, but which is now the property of the Earl of Kenmare.

The narrow passage or channel, between the upper and the other lakes, is at least five miles in length; and offers a charming variety of scenery. Indeed, I doubt whether anything about Killarney, surpasses the scene around Dinas Island. It is a perfect specimen of close river scenery; nor have I any recollection of having seen its equal on the banks of any of the many Continental rivers which are familiar to me.

Turc lake, which is reached after passing through the channel, is not at the first glance, so attractive as either of the other lakes; but if the traveller do not coast round Turc lake, he will lose much. It has numerous tiny bays and coves, — beautiful in form, — and offering to the eye of the painter, the most exquisite combination of colour; arising from the union of rock and foliage, and from the infinite variety of fern, lichens, and mosses, that overspread its banks.

The lower lake is preferred by some, to the two others; and although I do not coincide in this opinion, I willingly concede to it, merits of a very high order. Its chief character is beauty; and certainly a spot of more loveliness than Glena, it would be difficult to find. It is a little cove, at the head of the lower lake; and here Lady Kenmare has built her a pleasure house, on a gentle swell, with the freshest of verdure, and the sweetest of shrubs and flowers around; and set, like an emerald, in the bosom of deep towering woods. Another cottage, at a little distance, has been erected by Lord Kenmare, for the use of strangers; and although I am rather inclined to look upon a picnic as a good dinner spoiled; yet, in such a spot as this, the calamity might be endured.

One of the most beautiful islands on any of the lakes, or, I might perhaps say, on any lake, is Innisfallen. Never saw I such ash-trees as are here, — never such magnificent hollys. A walk round this little paradise well repays one. Although the island contains scarcely twenty acres, it offers a wonderful variety of scenery: little emerald lawns — forest glades in miniature — sylvan amphitheatres — groves, bowers, and thickets of evergreens, and flowering shrubs — and magnificent single trees, worthy of a primeval forest. There is an old ruin too, on the island, and a banqueting-house erected for the accommodation of strangers; and, when I saw it, it was prepared for a banquet. Lord Kenmare is the owner of Innisfallen; and also of Ross Island, another large and beautiful island on the lower lake. In speaking of Killarney, I must not forget its echoes. I had the advantage of having, in my boat, the Prince of Killarney bugle men, and I had also a cannon of a larger calibre than the public boats carry; and, in the course of our voyage, we often woke the echoes of the hills, and I never heard echoes in greater perfection. There is, certainly, something bordering on the sublime, in the oft-repeated echoes of the mountains, even when these are awoke, not by the deep-mouthed thunder, but by the sonorous bugle. The hills seem, alike, to call to each other; and, although it would have puzzled Burke[2] to trace the emotion of sublimity to terror, it may be traced to its truer origin — power; for — when we hear the call repeated and answered, from mountain to mountain — sometimes loud, and without interval, and then fainter and fainter — and, after a solemn pause, again rising, as if from some far distant glen — our imagination endues the mountains with life; and to their attributes of magnitude, and silence, and solitude, we, for a moment, add the power of listening, and a voice.

It will not be irrelevant, to say a few words in this place, of the comparative merits of the English and the Irish lakes.

Although the lakes of Killarney are three in number, yet they are all contained in one mountain hollow; and certainly there is not, within the same compass, anything in England presenting the same concentration of charms. There is infinitely greater variety at Killarney. In form, and in the outline of its mountain boundaries, the lower lake of Killarney is decidedly superior to Winandermere:

---

[2] The distinction between horror and terror and their relationship to the sublime was a topic that interested Gothic writer Ann Radcliffe and Edmund Burke, [Clachan ed.].

and although the head of Ulleswater presents a bolder outline than is anywhere to be found at Killarney; yet it is upon this outline alone, that the reputation of Ulleswater depends. Elsewhere than at Patterdale, the lake scenery is tame; and the same may be said of Winandermere; which, towards its lower extremity, is almost devoid of attraction. On the contrary, throughout the whole chain of lakes, there is a variety at Killarney: tameness is nowhere to be found; and I cannot think that the somewhat nearer approach to sublimity which is found at the head of Ulleswater, can weigh in the balance against the far greater variety in the picturesque and the beautiful, which Killarney affords. It would be unfair to compare the lakes of Killarney, with Winandermere, Keswick, and Ulleswater; for these are spread over a great extent of country; whereas, the lakes of Killarney are all contained within a smaller circumference than Winandermere: but even if such a comparison were to be admitted, Killarney would out-vie the English lakes in one charm, in which they are essentially deficient. I mean, the exuberance and variety of foliage which adorns both the banks and the islands of the Killarney lakes. Such islands as Ronan's Island, Oak Island, Dinas Island, and Innisfallen, covered with magnificent timber and gigantic evergreens, are nowhere to be found amongst the English lakes. I think it will be gathered from what I have said, that I accord the preference to Killarney.

No one must visit Killarney, without seeing Muckross Abbey. It is a very beautiful and very perfect remain, — and contains within it, the most gigantic yew tree I have ever seen. Its arms actually support the crumbling wall, and form a canopy above the open cloisters: the trunk of this majestic yew, measures thirteen feet in circumference. I was somewhat shocked with the want of propriety observed in the management of this spot. Human skulls in hundreds, and bones in thousands, are heaped in every corner; and at each step, it is more than likely, that one will kick some eyeless relic of mortality. The domain of Muckross is beautiful: it lies along the shores of the lower lake, and its shady walks are adorned by innumerable blossoming shrubs; amongst others, the rose of Sharon, and the gum-cistus.

The domain of the Earl of Kenmare is altogether lovely. Its lake and mountain views, and vistas, are beyond praise. I think I have never beheld any thing more captivating, than the vista from the dining-room windows: when the declining sun, streaming from above the mountain tops, falls slanting on the lake, and on the bright velvet lawn that stretches to its shore.

Peasantry in Killarney

CHAPTER III.

Kerry, Killorglin, Cahir-siveen, Valencia Island, Dingle

Journey through the Wilds of Kerry — Castlemain Bay — Killorglin — Lord Headly's Estate — Sea Views — O'Connell's Country — The Agitator in his own Country — The Grand Jury Bill — An Anecdote — Cahir-siveen — Condition of the Landholders — Intelligence of the Kerry Peasantry — Examples — Valentia Island — Voyage across the Bay of Dingle — Dingle, and the Condition of the People — Peculiarities of the Inhabitants of this district — Extreme early Marriages — The Catholic Clergy, and proposed Provision for them — Brandon Bay — The Tithe Question — Journey to Tralee.

My course now lay through the wilds of Kerry; and first, to Cahir-siveen, and Valentia Island; which, with the exception of the little islands called the Blaskets, is the nearest point of Ireland to the coast of America. The distance from Killarney to Cahir-siveen, which, on the maps, is generally marked Cahir, is about forty English miles, and the road is altogether a very interesting one; both on account of the scenery through which the traveller passes, and on account of the peculiarities that attach to the people of these parts, which are said to have been colonized by Spanish settlers, and which long held a close intercourse with the Peninsula.

The first few miles of the road, I had already passed over, in exploring the beauties of Killarney; and till reaching Milltown, there is not much to interest the traveller, excepting the glimpses of the lakes, which are caught from every eminence one passes. Milltown is a very poor town; the property of Sir George Godfrey; who, from all that I could learn, has more the will than the power of benefiting it. Beyond Milltown, the view opens finely, over the upper part of Dingle Bay and Castlemain: and soon after, I reached the town of Killorglin; the property of the Mullins' family, — and a still poorer place than Milltown. Beyond this town, the road continually increases in interest. The Iveragh range of mountains rises boldly on the left; and a lake, called Lough Carracht, is seen with one end buried among the steeps, and the other, approaching near to the road. A little farther on, the road enters and traverses for several miles, an extensive bog, also the property of the Mullins, or Ventry family. I never saw a bog better situated for improvement: it lies close to the bay of Dingle, and at a considerable elevation above it; and at the distance of but a few miles, there is a plentiful supply of limestone; and abundance of sea-sand close at hand. Yet, with the exception of that part of the bog which belongs to Judge Dey, it is entirely neglected, and nearly profitless. Judge Dey has the universal character of being an excellent and enterprising landowner; and, judging by what I saw, I have no doubt, that if this bog were all his property, it would long ago have been covered with luxuriant crops of grain and potatoes. It is on this road also, where lies that estate of Lord Headly, — so well known by the evidence of Mr. Nimmo, before the House of Commons[3]. The exertions made to reclaim that land, and the success which attended them, have been so fully detailed in that evidence, that any imperfect notices of mine are unnecessary. I saw land, which had formerly owned but the dominion of the sea, bearing fine crops of every description; and I saw a population, which before the exertions of Lord Headly, was little removed from savage, comfortably housed and clothed, and exhibiting more certain indications of civilization, than are often to be met in the most fertile and central parts of Ireland. In a little bay here, Lord Headly has erected some neat bathing cottages, which are much frequented during the summer. His lordship has an extensive property in this neighbourhood; and it everywhere exhibits those symptoms of improvement which might be expected.

Nothing can be finer than the road skirting the sea, after leaving Lord Headly's property. In the magnificence of its mountain and sea views, it is little inferior to any of the celebrated roads which have been constructed along the shores of the Mediterranean; and

[3] Positive reports of improvements in Lord Headley estate of Glenbeg were made in the *Report of the Select Committee on the State of the Poor in Ireland*, 1830, [Clachan ed.].

is every way superior to the road from Bangor to Conway, in North Wales. I am sorry I cannot say so much for the population and their dwellings. I never passed more wretched cabins, than on some part of this road. Some of the worst of these, are situated on the property of Lord Lansdowne, but are held under his lordship, by middle-men.

I was now in O'Connell's country: here was the property of Daniel O'Connell, Esq., or the Liberator, as the people called him; there, the property of Charles O'Connell, Esq.; and there again, the property of another O'Connell but the greater part of the O'Connell property — almost all that of *the* O'Connell, is held under head landlords; and he, is only an extensive middle-man. Near to Cahir-siveen, is the birth-place of the great agitator. It is a ruined house, situated in a hollow near to the road; and when I reached the spot, the driver of the car pulled up, and inquired whether I would like to visit the house. But the driver of my car, was not a native of these parts; for be it known to the reader, that O'Connell is less popular in his own country than he is elsewhere. If you ask an innkeeper, or an innkeeper's wife, any where in O'Connell's district, what sort of a man their landlord is? "Och, and sure he's the best o' landlords! — he takes the childer by the hand, and he wouldn't be over proud to dthrink tay with the landlady." But if you step into a cabin, the holder of which owns Daniel O'Connell, Esq., as his landlord; and if you ask the same question, he'll scratch his head, and say little any way. Shortly before I visited Cahir-siveen, there was a road-presentation in that neighbourhood, and the rate payers, who have now a vote in these matters, refused at first to pass it, unless the O'Connells would pay two-thirds of the expense; because, said they, "the O'Connells have lived long enough out of road presentations!!"

As I have mentioned this subject, I will add, that I have reason to know, from unquestionable authority, that before the late Grand Jury Bill was enacted — that is, up to the present time — there had been much shameful grand jury jobbing in many of the Irish counties; particularly in Tipperary, Clare, Limerick, Kerry, and Roscommon. A grand juror of Tipperary called one morning, previous to the holding of the quarter sessions, upon a brother grand juror — a man, however, of much greater influence than himself, — and pulling out, and unfolding voluminous plans and papers, began to explain the advantages which would accrue to the public, from the construction of a certain road through his, the expounder's property. "Put your papers in your pocket, man," said the man of influence; "say nothing about the public advantage. I'll just say it's a little job of my own;" and so things were managed. There can be no doubt that, in some respects, the Bill will work most advantageously for the public service, and most fatally for jobbers. It cannot be denied, however, that there will be exceptions from its benefits. A few days later, when I was at Tralee, a presentment account was opposed by several magistrates, on the ground that the road had not been repaired as it ought to have been; that the money had been mis-spent, and that the road was at that moment in a bad condition. The rate payers, however, being the majority, passed the account: because, said they, although the road might not be good enough for their Honours' springed carriages, it answered very well for them. Neither has the late Act at all removed the evils of the Grand Jury Assessment. There is great and manifest injustice in many provisions of the Grand Jury Assessment Act; and particularly in this, — that the expense of permanent improvements are laid upon the occupier of the land, and not upon the owners.

I reached O'Connell's town, Cahir-siveen, in time for an excellent fish dinner of haddock, and mullet; and the three or four hours that intervened between dinner and bed time, I spent in rambling about the environs of the village, and in the neighbouring country. The town is said to be rather improving; though, from its situation, I cannot think the improvement can ever be great; for it lies within a very dangerous navigation, high up the stream, that there forms an inlet of the sea; and in strong westerly winds, the only safe entrance, between the mainland and Valentia Island, is all but inaccessible.

The country around Cahir-siveen is extremely wild, and but very partially reclaimed: and the condition of the people far from being comfortable. I visited several wretched cabins, and found the inmates paying exorbitant rents. Land is not let here by the acre;

but by the quantity of land fit to support a cow. I found one man owning land for six cows, paying at the rate of 50s. per cow; and at that time, the price of butter was such, that not more than 40s. could be got for the produce of each cow. Others, I found paying in precisely the same proportion. The greater industry of the people — and, I may add, the greater intelligence, universal among the Kerry peasantry, — help them with their indifferent bargains. I saw in many of their cabins, beautiful examples of industry — every branch of a family occupied in doing something useful; and I did not address one individual, from whom I did not receive answers, that would have done credit to persons of any education; and yet, on asking one individual who had conversed with me readily and sensibly upon many subjects, how many weeks there were in a month, — I was answered, that there were two. Nature has done much for these people — education little.

Walking along a mountain path, I overtook a girl of about fourteen or fifteen years old — I speak by guess, for it is rarely in this country, that a girl can tell her age. She carried a basket, in which were from four to five dozen of eggs. I asked where she had got the eggs? — She had been round the country buying them cheap. Where was she taking them to? — She was going to send them, and some dozens more, with Mich O'Sullivan's carts, to Cork — Upon whose account was she buying the eggs? — On her own. On her own account? — Yes. Who gave her the money? — The parson (she was a Protestant) had lent it to her: some time ago, her cousin had sent a basket of eggs with Mich O'Sullivan, to Cork, and he had made three shillings. This was certainly a curious example of enterprise and industry. I returned into the town with the girl, and saw her father: he was a small landholder; and he said, Biddy went, after her day's work was done, and merchandized for herself.

The views about Cahir-siveen are interesting — of a wild and solitary character. The mountains jut into the sea on every side; the island of Valentia lies opposite, separated from the main land, by a narrow channel; and the small town, enclosed among the brown mountain slopes, seems like a place at the world's end.

The next day I visited Valentia Island: but my visit to it was a hurried one; for the navigation of Dingle Bay is safe only in fine weather; and being anxious to reach Ennis at the opening of the Clare assizes, it was necessary that I should take advantage of the favourable weather to cross the bay to Dingle. A great part of Valentia Island, is under tillage; and there is a considerable range of pasture. The houses of the tenants, I found of a superior description; but their internal comforts scarcely corresponded; for land is high let. Nearly all, if not all the island, belongs to the Knight of Kerry, who is much respected in this neighbourhood; and who has done considerable service to the place — not so much by outlay of money, as by example, in various modes of improvement. The slate quarry on the island is extensive and valuable, and is at present in the Knight of Kerry's own hands; and is worked for export. It is used for flagging, for fish slabs, and for many purposes to which marble has been usually applied; and finds a ready market in England. Several good houses are scattered over Valentia Island, besides those of the farmers. The house of the knight is situated near to the sea, on an eminence, on the east side of the island, and near to a little glen, and small rivulet.

I returned from Valentia Island to Cahir-siveen, just in time to save the tide, and embarked in a heavy fishing-boat, which was about to return to Dingle. With a smart breeze the voyage may be accomplished in two hours, but I had no such good fortune. There was scarcely a breath of wind, and we were forced to row the whole way; sometimes, indeed, profiting by the brief course of a passing breeze to hoist our sail; but losing more than we gained, by the suspension of rowing. This must, indeed, be a frightful navigation, with a heavy rolling sea before an Atlantic north-wester; and, being only desirous of reaching Dingle before night-fall, I did not regret the slowness of our progress, and the tranquility of the sea, which encouraged a more leisurely observation of the fine scenery that lay on every side. The tide did not permit us to steer directly for Dingle; and, accordingly, we made the opposite shore, considerably to the west, and then rowed under the rocks, eastward, passing in succession, Ventry Harbour, numerous bold headlands, and singularly formed rocks, and many curious sea-worn caves, never visited but by the sea-fowl, that are congregated in thousands along this coast, — riding on the wave, covering the rocks, and wheeling on the sides of the cliffs. I noticed many varieties of sea-fowl: some were of the purest white; some were white, all but the tips of the wings; and some were speckled-bodied, with red feet and bills.

Dingle harbour is what sailors call a blind harbour; that is, a harbour that, from the sea, is not discovered to be a harbour. It is exceedingly difficult to make this haven during a strong westerly wind; and vessels passing it by, and running to the eastward, are infallibly lost on Castlemain bar. When once entered, however, Dingle harbour is a very secure one. A vessel of six hundred tons' burden may go up to the pier, with a spring tide; and vessels of any tonnage may find secure anchorage within the inlet.

The town of Dingle is situated on the slope of the hills, with fine, and very high mountains round it on all sides, excepting one, where the sea forms a large inland lake. It is rather a good-looking town. The number of respectable houses is much greater than one would expect to find in so small and remote a place; and good gardens are generally attached to them; so that, viewed from a distance, the town appears to be well screened with wood. But Dingle is not a flourishing town. A thriving linen trade was once carried on here; and no trade is so beneficial as this, in giving employment to different descriptions of persons. But this trade is entirely fallen, and has not been replaced by any other. There is however, a considerable and an increasing export trade in corn and butter. About ten cargoes, averaging each two hundred tons, leave Dingle yearly, with corn and butter, for British ports. The town enjoys also a tolerable retail trade. The neighbouring country, as well as Cahir-siveen, and the opposite side of the bay, are supplied from Dingle; and one or two dealers lay in their stocks themselves, direct from England. There is also a considerable fishery at Dingle: — upwards of fifty fishing boats, with about 350 men, afford the means of support to about 1200 persons. Dingle supplies Tralee market with the finer kinds of fish; and fish-hucksters traffic regularly, with horses, between Dingle and Tralee.

I found a considerable number of unemployed persons in and about Dingle, and labour extremely cheap. Sixpence a day, and seven-pence at most, is the usual rate without diet; and it is the universal practice, in this part of the country, to work, during the summer, from five in the morning until seven in the evening. The provisions of the poor, however, are cheap here. I found potatoes only 2¼d. a stone.

The land around Dingle is in a very indifferent condition, as regards the occupiers. A great part of it is the property of the Mullins' family, held under a trust, created by a former Lord Ventry, and is badly managed. Tenants occupy miserably small lots; and being unable to live on the produce of their land, go, half the year, a begging, or in search of employment. Fuel, too, is scarce in this country; but the facility of catching fish perhaps counterbalances this disadvantage.

The Peninsula, or stripe of land, reaching from Tralee, westward, to the Atlantic, of which Dingle is the chief town, is said to have been colonized from Spain; and, in many respects, the people yet retain strong traces of their origin. Here, we see women with dark hair and jet black eyes — and dark brown-headed boys, that might have served as a study for Murillo — and men, whose gait and complexion only require to be set off by a Spanish hat, jacket, and girdle, to pass for bandits of Andalusia. Nor is the resemblance visible only in the aspect of the people: I fancied I discovered more pride, and more reserve; and, in a quarrel which I chanced to see, there was less vociferation, and, as it seemed to me, a graver deportment than I had elsewhere observed. But this might possibly be fancy: it is certain, however, that the features of many of the people are decidedly Spanish; and in the names of places, a Spanish origin may often be traced.

Marriages in this district are contracted at an earlier age than in any part that I had yet visited. Fourteen and thirteen, are common ages for the marriage of girls; fifteen is not considered at all an early age for marriage; and there are even instances of their having been contracted at so early an age as twelve. This is, on many accounts, a great and public evil: and, among the benefits which might be expected to be derived from the assignment, under cautious regulation, of some government provision for the Catholic clergy, the discouragement of early marriages would certainly be one. It is well known that marriage is among the most fruitful sources of profit to the priest; and if the abolition of baptismal and marriage dues were made consequent upon such a provision as I have alluded to, it would be no longer the interest of the priest to encourage, or countenance — as it is certain he often does — the unwise, and almost criminally early marriages of the peasantry. I am far from meaning to say that such encouragement is universal; I know, however, that it is frequent; and the Catholic priest, who betters his condition by the marriages of his flock, would be committing an act of rare virtue were he not merely neutral, but were even to discourage early marriage. At all events, it appears to me, that men's interests ought never to be placed in opposition to the public good; and that — if legislation can prevent this — legislators are bound to apply the remedy. I will mention another advantage which would certainly result from such a provision for the Catholic clergy. It would encourage a more respectable class of men to become members of the priesthood; and this would essentially contribute towards the peace of the country. The warmest defenders of the Catholic clergy would admit, that many, are utterly disqualified from exercising judiciously, and in a spirit suited to the times, the functions of their calling, owing to the sphere of life from which they have been taken: and, that some certain provision, by way of glebe, or otherwise, would tempt a better order of men to enter the priesthood, cannot I think admit of the smallest doubt. I may probably again recur to this subject: at present, I shall only add, that I would look for benefit from the provision alluded to, rather in its results upon early marriage, and in the encouragement it would give to a better order of clergy, than in the effect which some suppose it would have, in diminishing the influence of the priesthood.

The inns, in this part of the country, put me in mind of those I had seen in the Engadine. The houses are very spacious; and the keeping of the inn is only one branch of the business of the innkeeper. Both at Cahir-siveen, and at Dingle, the inn-keeper kept an extensive shop for the sale of groceries, and of all kinds of cloth and haberdashery goods.

Before leaving Dingle, I crossed the mountains to the heights above Brandon Bay, which lies on the north side of the Peninsula. It was a long and fatiguing ascent; but it was repaid by the very striking and extensive view from Connor's Hill, from which you look down upon the sea on both aides: the view on one side embracing Dingle Bay, as far as Valentia Island, with the town and fine harbour immediately below; and on the other side, comprehending Brandon Bay, and various fine headlands, with high mountains on both sides, and deep and wide mountain valleys; and innumerable tarns, dark and still, lying in the hollows of the hills; and distant cascades, and nearer torrents; and all, in short, that lends interest to mountain scenery.

Returning from this excursion, I remarked some bog land brought newly into a state of partial cultivation; and upon making some inquiries, I was told that this was done, because no tithe would in future be exigible from it. There and everywhere I have yet travelled, I have found the tithe question a difficult one to grapple with. Utterly and at once to extinguish tithes, every one in Ireland admits, would be only making a present to the landlord; and any adjustment that leaves it in the landlord's power to shift the burden from himself, would confer little benefit on those for whom it is intended. Even, however, if the landlord should succeed in laying the addition upon the rent, it is better that the tenant should pay the charges upon his possession in a lump, than by separate demands: and that all the charges should be exigible by the landlord: a farmer could better calculate the amount he had to pay; and would know when to be prepared; and as it cannot be the true interest of the landlord unnecessarily to distress a good tenant, more indulgence might in general be expected from him, than from the inexorable tithe-proctor.

After spending an interesting day or two at Dingle, I left it for Tralee. The road traverses the mountains, diagonally from the Dingle, to the Tralee side; and leads the traveller through an improving country, and through scenery of a highly attractive character. Several inconsiderable villages are passed through: a gap, far superior to the gap of Dunlow, is seen on the left, with a fine lake half hidden in it; and from the summit of the mountain ridge, a splendid prospect opens over Tralee Bay, across to Kerry Head, and the Shannon Mouth. I reached Tralee a little before dusk, and found the streets and every inn crowded, — for the quarter sessions had opened the day before: but I succeeded in finding comfortable lodgings.

CHAPTER IV.

Tralee, Listowel and Tarbert, Ennis

Tralee — The Quarter Sessions in Tralee — The Civil and Criminal Cause List — State of Kerry — Faction — The Police of Ireland — Litigiousness of the Irish — Prosperity of Tralee Trade — Prices of Provisions — Unemployed Poor — Journey to Listowel and Tarbert — Traits of Character — First View of the Shannon — Details — Tarbert, and the Shores of the Shannon — Irish Inns of the West — Steam Navigation on the Shannon — Ascent of the Shannon to Limerick — Road to Ennis — Clare, and the River Fergus — Ennis — Land, and High Rents — Environs of Ennis.

I have no hesitation in pronouncing Tralee, the county town of Kerry, to be altogether the most thriving town I have seen since leaving Clonmel; and, in some respects, it leaves Clonmel behind it. Tralee has streets that would not disgrace the best quarters of any city; and these, not streets of business, which it also has, — but streets containing gentlemen's houses, or, at all events, houses which no gentleman might be ashamed to live in.

I have said, that I arrived at Tralee when the quarter sessions were about to be held; and I did not neglect the opportunity afforded me: for, upon no occasion, is so much insight obtained at so small an expenditure of time and labour, into the character of the peasantry; and even into the state of the country. Being accommodated with a seat on the bench, I had better opportunity for observation, and for noting the proceedings.

The first thing that strikes a stranger, attending a court of this kind in Ireland, is, the military air of the place, — the armed police in military uniform, guarding the avenues, and stationed throughout the court. The next thing that strikes one, is the intense interest that seems to be excited among the people. But I soon found, that there were other and more important subjects of wonder than these. This was a quarter session for one half of the county of Kerry; and can the reader guess how many civil causes were to be disposed of? There were *fourteen hundred and seventy causes* entered for judgment; and the assistant barrister informed me, that this was not considered a heavy list. Seventy-seven of this number were ejectments; and the tremendous remainder was chiefly made up of breaches of contract, — indicating, I fear, at the same time, a woeful lack of veracity and just dealing; and a most indomitable spirit of litigiousness.

Nor was I less struck, nor do I believe the reader will be less struck, with the list of criminal cases handed to me. The following was the classification: — .

Assault	47
Riotous Assembly	74
Aggravated Assault	1
Rescue	34
Rescue Decree	21
Larceny	10
Embezzlement	4
Taking and retaining forcible possession	4
Libel	1
Injury to the Freehold	3
In all	199

One hundred and ninety-nine criminal cases at a quarter sessions, for one half of the remote and quiet county of Kerry!! and of these, *one hundred and seventy-four* cases implying the undue exercise of physical force!! But it is necessary that I should here enlarge a little. In England, when we speak of a disturbed county, we mean, a county in which there are movements directed to some particular purpose, — or arising out of opposition to some particular law, — or insurrectionary movements; and I have not the least doubt, that if, in Parliament, the condition of the west of Ireland were spoken of, it would be said to be perfectly tranquil; and we might, probably, have tirades against the large and expensive police establishment kept up in a quiet country, of which the county of Kerry might be cited as an example. But to call a county quiet, in one half of which, during three months, there have been seventy-four examples of riotous assembly, and fifty-five cases of rescue[4], — together with nearly fifty cases of personal assault, is a perversion of words. These assemblies are not, indeed, assemblies of white-feet, or peep-of-day boys; nor are they directed against the collection of tithes, — or of rent, — nor have in view any express political purpose; — and so far, indeed, they are less important than if they had any of these objects; — but they are riots for all that, — disturbances of the peace, — assemblages of persons who fight with each other, and maim each other, and kill each other; and no one, but through the grossest ignorance of Ireland, or to serve party purposes, would speak of the present police of Ireland, otherwise than in terms of the highest commendation, and as a force at present absolutely requisite to prevent the complete disorganization of society — even if there were no agitators, and Ireland had no elements of political or agrarian agitation. I have no hesitation in saying, that for putting down these private factions, out of which arise the disgraceful and savage brutalities, that are often perpetrated by wholesale, legislation is just as requisite as it is for any more specific purpose. These factions, which are not understood in England, create far more disturbance, and far more bloodshed, than any of the associations entered into for illegal purposes. I was in this county at the time of the memorable affair of Ballybunion, when nearly two score persons were driven into the Shannon, and drowned, and knocked on the head like so many dogs; and will anybody say, that premeditated fights of this kind, solemnly resolved upon months before, do not require as vigorous an intervention of the law, as any disturbance arising out of a tithe distraining[5]! Where magistrates are afraid to act, and witnesses dare not swear; and where, in one reputed quiet county, more riots, attended with loss of life, take place in one month, than in all England and Scotland for a year, it is surely idle to talk of the expense of a police.

---

[4] Possibly meaning to take forcible possession of something, [Clachan ed.].

[5] Taking a debtor's property as payment, [Clachan ed.].

But let me observe, that the causes of these disturbances are the same as those which answer to the call of political agitation — imperfect civilization, and want of employment. Education, employment for the people, and a vigorous administration of the law, will dissolve the elements of these, as well as of all disturbance; and although at this moment, a strong police is absolutely requisite to maintain in Ireland anything like order and decorum, I have as little doubt, that healing measures, coupled with an extensive and practicable system of education, will gradually diminish the necessity for coercion of any kind. Let government continue to act with moderation; let the tithe question be settled; let the extremes of all parties be discouraged; let Irish interests be not sacrificed to a too paltry economy; let the infirm and the aged poor be cared for; let the superabundant labour of Ireland be thrown upon her wastes; let public works be encouraged; let agitation for all dishonest purposes, be firmly met, and agitators scorned; let the church be wisely, but thoroughly reformed; let, in short, the government continue to show — what the people of England already give it credit for — a sympathy with the real evils of the country, and a determination, — spite of landlords, — spite of church dignitaries — spite of agitators of all kinds — to do justice; let all this be, and Ireland will continue but a little while longer, the distracted, poverty-stricken, crushed, and unhappy land, which a century of neglect and misgovernment has made it.

The litigiousness of the Irish peasantry is most remarkable; and I am inclined to think that litigiousness is encouraged by the frequency of holding sessions. Law seems to be always at hand; and it accustoms the people too much to these exhibitions; it is a fact, that were petty sessions have been made less frequent, the quantity of business has greatly diminished. A calculation was made for me, by a gentleman well acquainted with these matters, of the number of cases of all kinds tried in the county of Kerry during a year; and upon a fair average of cases tried at each of the petty sessions and manor courts, the whole number amounted to the enormous sum of 33,000. Wherever I have seen the quarter sessions in Ireland, it has impressed me favourably; and I doubt whether the contemplated alterations will be beneficial. I am strongly inclined to be of opinion, however, that the peace of Ireland would be greatly preserved by the establishment of a paid magistracy. Local connection is inimical to the steady and fearless administration of justice; and it is a fact, that strangers, brought into office as police inspectors, have more influence among the people, and can effect more, than the magistrates who have been always resident among them.

The indications of prosperity visible in the outward appearance of Tralee, I found upon inquiry, to be just indications. Twenty years ago, Tralee was little else than a congregation of cabins; and within a far shorter period, it has received, — as a merchant of the town expressed it, — its new face.

From September, 1833, till May, 1834 (eight months), 4000 tons of wheat were exported from Tralee, 3000 tons of oats, and 400 tons of barley. Besides this very considerable quantity there was bought in the market for home consumption, 1000 tons of wheat, 70 tons of oats, and 4000 tons of barley. Since the year 1825, the corn export trade of Tralee has increased about one-third; and the home trade, about one-fifth. The butter export trade of Tralee used to be considerable; but it is greatly on the decline, — scarcely one-twentieth part of the quantity being now exported, comparatively with the year 1825.

The retail trade of Tralee is an extensive and improving one; and many of the dealers are wealthy. As good shops are to be found in Tralee, as in Cork; and the stock, in many of them, is very extensive. A ship canal is now constructing from the bay to the town; but its probable utility is doubted by many. It is thought that the strong westerly gales, which blow into the bay, will accumulate sand in the canal, and obstruct navigation.

I was at Tralee on market day, and I never recollect to have seen a busier place. Independently of an extensive supply of country produce, there was a very abundant exhibition of all kinds of manufactured goods, and apparel; and every shop in the town was crowded to the door.

The following are the prices of some articles of provision in Tralee. Beef, averages 3d. per lb.; mutton, 3½d.; pork, 2d.; a fine turkey, in the season, costs 1s. 9d.; a fine goose, 10d.; and fine fowls, 8d. a couple; a good codfish can be bought for about 8d.; and oysters are 3d. a dozen; potatoes, when I was at Tralee, in the scarce season, were 3d. per stone. Servants' wages are very low in this neighbourhood. A man servant does not receive more than £8, and a female servant never more than £3, and often as little as £2, and even 30s. House-rent in Tralee is high, — higher than in any English county town: but, a little way out of Tralee, it is moderate enough. A gentleman, whom I visited, had an excellent house, somewhat more than two miles from Tralee, beautifully situated on the bay, with spacious out-houses, and with ten English acres of good land, for which he paid £45. Estimating the land at £2 10s. per acre, (for land around Tralee lets high), he paid £20 for his house and its accommodations.

The town of Tralee is the property of Sir Edward Denny; he grants leases on lives, renewable for ever; but it is not in his power to let ground at a lower rate than £10 an acre. He is also the chief proprietor of the surrounding country; but the occupying tenants chiefly hold under middle-men, who extract the utmost rent that competition can produce. I will take this opportunity of saying, that a gradual reduction of rents in Ireland, is to be expected from the system now so general among landowners, of getting quit of middle-men at expired leases. Landlords, I think, are beginning to see their interest more clearly in this matter; and if, as I earnestly hope may speedily be the case, some legislative enactment compels, or at least encourages, the cultivation of waste lands, and the employment of the able-bodied labourer on public works, competition for land will gradually diminish; and rents will at length find their just level.

I found at Tralee, a greater number of unemployed poor, than from the prosperity of the town, I could have expected. But the recent improvements in building houses, and in the erection of a new court-house, which is every way a handsome and commodious structure, attracted a large supply of labour to the town; and these being now almost completed, the demand has ceased. The canal indeed, employs many; but wages are extremely low; and in this rainy climate, it often happens that the labourers, after working in the canal from five in the morning until eleven in the forenoon, are discharged for the day with the pittance of twopence; and thus, these men and their families, are made paupers for that day.

There is a spa in the neighbourhood of Tralee, considerably resorted to for its waters; the situation of the place is pleasant; and a number of pretty country houses have been erected in the vicinity.

It was the evening of market day when I left Tralee for Listowel. I was seated on the mail car; and as the streets were thronged with carts and people, a little boy marched before, blowing a trumpet; while the driver, with an air of extraordinary importance stood up in his seat, and from one end of the street to the other, bawled out to the "boys" and the "gintlemen" to make room for his majesty's mail coach.

The country between Tralee and Listowel is naturally fertile, with here and there some bog land, which might be made fertile. The children whom I saw standing about the cabin doors, or tending the pigs or goats, appeared altogether regardless of covering; several, I noticed with nothing but skirts; apparently unconscious that clothes were any comfort: and one boy, with neither shirt, nor any nether garments whatever — with nothing but a jacket, and a great rose stuck in the button-hole, could not but excite a smile.

Listowel is approached by crossing a long bridge over the river Feale. The town is but a poor one; but as it was late when I reached it, and not having it in my power to stay longer than that night, owing to the necessity of reaching Ennis, I had no leisure for inquiries.

I left Listowel at a very early hour, for Tarbert, that, if necessary, I might cross the Shannon into Clare the same day. An early journey sometimes shows a traveller what he could not see at a later hour. Some of the cabins by the way side were still closed; and the inmates of others had newly opened their doors. It was Sunday morning; and I observed that the articles of apparel meant to be displayed at mass, and which had been washed the night before, had been left on the hedges all night — a practice that speaks favourably for the honesty of the people. I observed also, that many of the Kerry peasantry in this district, were not so poor, as from the appearance of their cabins, one might have guessed them to be. Out of one cabin, a calf might be seen picking its way; a couple of goats issuing from another; while within, might be seen and heard, the cocks and hens, which had not yet been turned out to earn their day's bread.

It was this morning, that, for the first time, I saw that noblest of all rivers in the British European dominions — the Shannon. It was impossible to look upon the Shannon without feeling deeply interested; and this for many reasons. I knew it to be the greatest of all our rivers; I knew it to be a great artery, by means of which, improvement might be carried, and capital circulated, through the remotest parts of Ireland; I saw it to be in itself, a noble stream, rivalling the finest of the continental rivers; and an additional interest was communicated to it, from the belief that, to my countrymen, that part of Ireland lying to the west of the Shannon, is a *terra incognita*.

But as I shall, for some time, have frequent occasion to speak of the Shannon, and as it will be our companion during a considerable part of this journey, I will here speak a little more in detail of this noble river; and, in doing so, I shall not scruple to avail myself of the valuable information given by Mr. Williams[6], in a pamphlet published by him, upon the internal navigation of Ireland.

The source of the Shannon is reputed to be Loch Allen: but some say, and I have no doubt those who say so are right, that Loch Allen has its feeders, and they therefore, though incorrectly perhaps, place the source of the Shannon higher than Loch Allen. By and by, I shall visit Loch Allen, and shall probably then be able to tell more accurately which is the source of the Shannon. The course of the river is two hundred and thirty-four miles; and the most singular feature about this great river is, that throughout its whole course, it possesses a sufficient depth of water for the

---

[6] Charles Wye Williams, *Observations on the Inland Navigation of Ireland and the Want of Employment for Its Population: With a Description of the River Shannon*, London: Vacher, 1833, [Clachan ed.].

purposes of internal intercourse. With some trifling interruptions, it is navigable from its mouth to its source, The other singular characteristic of this river is, its extraordinary diversity. It is partly river, and partly lake. In the upper part of its course, it expands into two great lakes, Lough Derg, and Lough Ree, each of them twenty miles in length, — and forms, in its course from Leitrim to Limerick, many smaller lakes, varying from one to three miles in length. Below Limerick, to the sea, a distance of sixty miles, it forms a magnificent estuary, varying in breadth, from one to eight miles, and capable of bearing to the quay of Limerick, a vessel of 400 tons burden. The whole fall of the river amounts to 146 feet 10 inches. Mr. Williams says, "From the circumstance of the Shannon running through the centre of the kingdom, it may be compared, for the purposes of intercourse, to double that length of coast."

The Shannon washes the shores of no fewer than ten counties, — Leitrim, Roscommon, Longford, Westmeath, King's County, Galway, Tipperary, Clare, Limerick, and Kerry.

"How," says Mr. Williams, "can we convey to English eyes, the picture of the Shannon through its great course?" The fact is there is nothing more required than to glance at a good map of Ireland in order to obtain a tolerable notion of the nature and extent of this noble river, and of its value, as a means of improvement. I trust the reader will become better acquainted with the Shannon, as he proceeds with me on my journey; and that when we stand together near to its source, we shall almost be able to write a pamphlet on it ourselves. Prefixed to the second volume of this work, a chart of the course of the Shannon, reduced from Mr. Williams' map, and with some additions of my own, will materially assist the reader.

It was on approaching Tarbert, that I ran into this digression on the Shannon. I now resume my narrative.

Tarbert is a very small town, situated at the head of a little bay of the Shannon, which, from the entrance to Tarbert Bay, to the nearest point of the opposite coast of Clare, is about two and a half miles abroad. Tarbert Bay is prettily wooded; and the banks of the river, below Tarbert, are adorned by several handsome seats. It was Sunday, and I had an opportunity of seeing the peasantry of this neighbourhood, with holiday looks, and holiday clothes. I saw more incongruity of apparel here, than I had anywhere else seen; and a greater partiality for gaudy colours. Red petticoats, and bright yellow shawls, were much in vogue; and so smart were the women's caps, that every hood was thrown back, to let them be seen. It was singular enough to see some tolerably neat holiday apparel, accompanied by bare feet and legs; I fear it was not the will that consented — for although it is no doubt often matter of choice to go barefooted, yet this certainly could not have been the case on Sunday.

I have already spoken of the goodness of the Irish inns. My remarks, however, were made before I had travelled into the remoter parts of the country; and when I remarked to any Irish person, that I had found the inns better than I expected, I was told to suspend my judgment until I had visited the less frequented parts of the country. I have now travelled through the remotest extremities of the wilds of Kerry; and I find no reason to retract the opinion I expressed. At Kenmare, at Cahir-siveen, at Dingle, at Listowel, and now at Tarbert, I found comfortable, and clean inns. I have at this inn, a well and newly carpeted room, with good mahogany chairs, three excellent mahogany tables, a handsome glass over the chimney piece, clean chintz window curtains, white blinds, and the walls of the room well papered. My bed-room is as unexceptionable; and every thing is comfortably served up at table. Prices continue nearly the same: dinner is generally charged 2s., tea 1s., breakfast 1s. 3d., bed 1s. 8d., and whiskey 5d. per glass, with water and sugar.

I spent the afternoon in walking five or six miles down the shore of the Shannon, as far as Ardmore point. The evening was remarkably fine, and the atmosphere clear; so that the whole of the opposite coast of Clare, as far as Kilrush, was beautifully distinct; and I was able even to see clearly, the round tower on Scattery Island.

The reader, probably, knows, that there is a steam navigation on the Shannon, both above and below Limerick. One of the

Company's vessels plies between Limerick and Kilrush, and takes passengers from Tarbert, if any there be; and I, of course, took advantage of it the next day, to go up to Limerick. In order to embark, it is necessary to walk to Tarbert Island, a mile distant; but there is some talk of constructing a pier, either at Tarbert, or at Glyn, a village a mile or two farther up the river. The fares on the Shannon are very moderate; the distance from Tarbert to Limerick, is thirty-five miles, and the fare is 4s. The vessels, too, are excellent, and in every way well appointed.

Soon after leaving Tarbert, the river contracts; for on the Clare side, a narrow headland pushes itself far into the river. The Clare side is here sloping and cultivated, without much wood, which is more abundant on the other side of the river; and on the Kerry side, the bank is also adorned by several villas. Two or three miles above Tarbert, we were opposite to Glyn village, and to the very handsome residence of the Knight of Glyn, with its fine woods around it. The village looks neat and clean from the water; and the church on a neighbouring height, is a very pretty object. Here, the county of Kerry ends, and Limerick county begins.

On the Clare side the river now forms a wide bay, called Labeshida Bay; and the banks, both on the Clare and Limerick side, exhibit the same features, until we reach Loghill. It is, I believe, on this part of the Shannon, that the real incidents which gave rise to the excellent novel, called "The Collegians,"[7] took place; and that the real Elie O'Connor was betrayed and drowned. On both sides, the banks of the Shannon are beautiful beyond Loghill. On the Limerick side, situated on a green eminence near to the river, is Mount Trenchard, the seat of Mr. Spring Rice; and opposite, on the Clare side, the beautiful domain of Cahircon, with its deep bay, and mansion buried among woods.

---

[7] Gerald Griffin's novel, *The Collegians*, London: Saunders & Otley 1829, was based on a real event involving the murder of a young wife by her husband because she would not be accepted by his family. It was the basis of *The Colleen Bawn*, or *The Brides of Garryowen* by Irish playwright Dion Boucicault, [Clachan ed.].

Soon after passing Mount Trenchard we reached Foynes Island, the property of Lord Dunraven; and immediately afterwards, Achnish Island, which however, is not an island, unless in extraordinarily high tides. These are both on the Limerick side of the river, which now, on the other side expands into the fine estuary, which reaches far into the county of Clare, and is studded with grassy islands of the most beautiful greenness, covered with innumerable cattle. The view was here most captivating. The deep woods of Cahircon and Mount Trenchard were behind; the green islands and more distant hills of Clare, on one side, with the estuary of the river Fergus stretching far to the left; while on the Limerick side, a recess in the banks shewed, at a little distance, the town and castle of Askeaton; and at a greater distance, "the Hill of Truth," so celebrated throughout this part of the country, as the resort of the fairies, or "good people." The view of this hill, gave rise to some conversation touching the good people; and the man at the helm, entertained his auditors with many stories of fairies, — in the existence of whom, he evidently entertained the firmest belief.

The river, after we passed the estuary of the Fergus, suddenly contracts to about a mile and a half wide; and Begh Castle, an old black ruin, and near to it, the domain of Castletown, and still farther, the fine ruin, called Carrig-aguinal Castle, situated on a bold rock, present themselves successively. These are all on the Limerick side; but on the side of Clare, the objects of attraction are still finer, — particularly Bunratty Castle; which, together with a new mansion, lies in a deep recess, surrounded by wood, and with fine green slopes behind.

All the remainder of the distance to Limerick, the views are full of beauty. High, sloping, and finely cultivated hills, a little back from the river; with handsome houses, and more than one old ruin nearer to the banks, are seen on the Clare side; while Cooper Hill, and Tervac, two fine domains, lie embosomed in wood on the other bank. The river has now gradually contracted; and the two last of its reaches, up to Limerick, are not more than from a quarter to three quarters of a mile in breadth. Limerick is not seen, until the last reach of the river be entered; and owing to the absence of spires and architectural eminences, the city does not shew to great advantage.

My object being to reach Ennis, the county town of Clare, about twenty-six miles from Limerick, I did little more than step out of the steam vessel, and into a car; and at present, therefore, I shall say nothing of the city, until my return from Ennis.

The first part of the road to Ennis, embraces nearly the same views as the voyage up the Shannon; for the road runs parallel to, though at a little distance from the river. From several of the eminences over which I passed, a great part of the course of the lower Shannon is laid open; and the country on either side of the road was green, fertile, and beautiful. Several of the ruins which are seen from the river, — particularly Bunratty Castle, — I passed close by; and several fine domains, — among others, that belonging to Sir Edward O'Brien, lay in our way.

The little town of Clare, which, from its situation ought to be the county town, in place of Ennis, lies between Limerick and Ennis, and only about two miles from the latter. There is a fine navigation up the estuary of the river Fergus, to the bridge of Clare; so that Clare is the export point of the Ennis market. A very trifling expenditure would extend the water communication to Ennis; and there is no doubt, that, in that event, the prosperity of the town would rapidly increase; for Clare is not only a fine corn country, but an extensive cattle-breeding country. The proposal of a canal, however, has met with every opposition from narrow-mindedness and jobbing. The great Ennis proprietor likes nothing that costs any thing; and the proprietor of Clare is not of course anxious to remove the point of export from Clare to Ennis. Notwithstanding the advantages possessed by Clare, the place looks poverty-stricken.

I reached Ennis just as it fell dark; and found the town in all the bustle that in an Irish county town, precedes the holding of assizes: the inns were all choke full; and for lodgings, the most exorbitant prices were demanded. From three to eight guineas, for a few days, were asked for two rooms; and I was glad to find a place to creep into, even on these terms. Although the assize was opened on the following day, no business was entered upon, until the day after; and I therefore employed the interval in those perambulations, scrutinies, and inquiries, which occupy a part of my attention in every town.

I had not yet seen, in Ireland, any town with suburbs so extensive, in comparison with the town itself; or, perhaps, it would be more correct to say, that I had not seen any town with so few good streets, in comparison with the bad; for the rows and streets of cabins form, in fact, the greater part of the town, and cannot properly be called suburbs. There is not, indeed, one good street in Ennis; and there are only two streets which rise above the rank of lanes. Ennis, however, is a populous town, containing 12,000 inhabitants; and is susceptible of considerable improvement in many ways, but especially by the construction of some communication with the river navigation at Clare.

The retail trade in Ennis is not extensive, excepting in the necessaries of life. Limerick is so near, and the communication with it so frequent and so easy, that it absorbs a great part of the retail trade of the county of Clare.

I have nowhere yet found land let dearer, or its small occupiers in a poorer condition, than in the neighbourhood of Ennis. I found average good land, but by no means first rate land, situated about a mile from the town, let at £7 and £8 per acre; and very indifferent land, as far and even at a greater distance from the town, let at £4 and £5 per acre. This is literally squeezing the uttermost farthing out of the soil; and the proprietor of a large portion of the land in this neighbourhood, a Mr. Gore, is one of those short-sighted individuals, whose object is, to keep up a nominal rent roll, and to let his land to the highest bidder. This gentleman takes no warning by the frequency of unpaid rents, and possessions relinquished; and finds no difficulty, in the present state of the country, when the demand for improved land is greater than the supply, of letting his land at whatever price he chooses to put upon it. The miserable suburbs of Ennis afford evidence of the same system. I need scarcely add, that there is great want of employment in and about Ennis; and that nothing is done in the way of providing it.

The country about Ennis offers many beautiful scenes. I would particularly name Eden vale and Eden lake, — spots of great loveliness and repose. But the neighbourhood of such charming scenes as these, too often remind one of Castle Rack-rent — a large neglected looking mansion, and a pack of hounds; and congregations of miserable cabins scattered around. Clare is a backward county; little has been done for it; and in no county, has grand-jury jobbing been more unblushingly carried on.

CHAPTER V.

Clare

Clare Assizes — English and Irish Assizes — Description of Cases tried — Fair Murders — Spirit of Faction — Difficulty of eliciting Truth — Disregard of an Oath — Extent to which Faction is carried — A paid Magistracy necessary — Rape Cases — Abduction — Murder — Assaults — Kissing the Book — Superstitions — General Impressions from attending an Irish Assize.

A small Irish county town, during assizes presents a spectacle that is never seen in England; for even supposing the calendar to be as long, in an English as in an Irish county, — which it never is, — the difference in the character of the cases to be tried, materially affects the aspect of the town and its population. In England, a case of murder or man-slaughter, brings to the county town only the near relations of the party to be tried, — and perhaps, of the party prosecuting; but in Ireland, things are on a different scale. The English murder is a private act, perpetrated by some ruffian for the sake of gain: the Irish homicide has been committed for no reason at all; and not by one cold-blooded ruffian, but by a crowd of demi-barbarians, who meet for the purpose of fighting; and who have no other reason for fighting, than because one half of the number are called O'Sullivan and the other O'something else: so that when a manslaughter is to be prosecuted at an Irish assize, the case does not bring up merely the accused and his one or two witnesses, but it brings half the "boys" in the county who bear the same name as the accused; and as many more, of the same name as the man who was killed, — every one of the former, ready to kiss the book, and swear, that the boy accused of the homicide, never handled a shillelah, or lifted a stone, or was seen in a "scrimmage" in his days; and every one of the latter as ready to swear, that the boy that was killed, was the most peaceable boy that ever bore his name, and that he was killed for no reason at all. Besides these homicides cases, which are peculiar to an Irish assize, prosecutions of any kind bring together a greater number of persons than in England, — for be it a robbery, or a rape, or any other crime, of which a man is accused, all his relations come forward to swear an alibi. It may be easily conceived, therefore, what a motley crowd fills the streets of an Irish county town at the time of an assize.

Nor is it only the number of persons, but their eagerness also, that strikes a stranger. Besides the groups that throng every part of the open streets, and who are always in earnest talk, dense crowds are collected at the door of every attorney's office, and no one of this brotherhood can walk a yard, without having his sleeve pulled by half-a-dozen "boys" or women, all interested for or against somebody; and entreating his honour to get them justice: which may mean, either to get a man hanged, or to save a man from hanging.

The most numerous class of cases at most Irish assizes, is that which is facetiously denominated *fair* murders; that is, homicides committed at fairs; and I do not know any means, by which so much insight is to be obtained into the character of the Irish peasantry, and into the condition of the country, and state of things among the lower classes of society, as by listening to these prosecutions *for fair* murders. There were many of these prosecutions at the Ennis assizes; and, although I had already heard much of the factions, into which the peasantry are divided, I had no conception of the extent of this evil, nor of the bitterness with which this spirit of faction is attended. However these factions may have originated, there is now no distinction among their adherents, excepting that which arises from the possession of a different name. The O'Sullivans are as distinct a people from the O'Neils, as the Dutch from the Belgians. The factions have chiefs, who possess authority. Regular agreements are made to have a battle; the time agreed upon is generally when a fair takes place; and, at these rights, there is regular marshalling, and "wheeling;" and, as for its being a crime to break a "boy's" head, such an idea never enters the brain of any one.

The spirit of faction is brought into court by almost every witness in these prosecutions. I saw a witness, a woman, brought in support of the prosecution for a homicide committed on some cousin, — who on being desired to identify the prisoners, and the court-keeper's long rod being put into her hand, that she might point them out, struck each of them a smart blow on the head. As for finding out the truth, by the mere evidence of the witnesses, it is generally impossible. Almost all worth knowing is elicited on the cross-examination: and it is always, by the appearance and manner of the witness, more than by his words, that the truth is to be gathered. All the witnesses, examined for the prosecution, were, by their own account, mere lookers on at the battle; nor stick, nor stone had they. *Their* party had no mind to fight that day; but, in making this assertion, they always take care to let it be known, that, if they had had a mind to fight, they could have handled their shillelahs to some purpose. On the other hand, all the witnesses for the prisoner aver just the same of themselves; so that it is more by what witnesses wont tell, than by what they do tell, that truth is discovered. Half the witnesses called, on both sides, have broken heads; and it is not unfrequently by a comparison of the injuries received on both sides, and by the evidence of the doctor, that one is helped to the truth.

It will be easily seen, from what I have said, that I found ample confirmation of what I had often heard, — the small regard for veracity among the Irish peasantry, and their general disregard of an oath. To save a relation from punishment, or to punish any one who has injured a relation, an Irish peasant will swear anything. This would be called, by some, hatred of the law; but, although, in swearing falsely, the Irish peasant wishes to defeat the ends of justice, he does not do so, merely because he hates justice and the law, but because he thinks he is bound to save his relation, or any one of his faction. If the name of the man who was killed be O'Grady, then every witness, who comes up to be sworn for the prosecution, is also an O'Grady; or, if they be women, they were O'Gradys before they were married; and, if the name of the prisoner be O'Neil, then all the witnesses, for the defence, are O'Neils; or, if there be any exceptions in name, still there is a relationship of some kind.

The factions, which occasion the atrocities of which we, in England, know very little, (for the cases reported from the Irish assizes, in the English papers, are, generally, cases in some degree political, and are seldom, or ever, the homicides arising out of fights at fairs), have never been energetically met by the law and the magistracy. Some years ago, when trading magistrates were common, their non-interference was purchased by services performed. If a magistrate, living in the vicinity of a place where two great factions wished to try their strength, had a meadow ready for mowing — or a field of wheat ripe for the sickle — or wished to lay in his winter's turf — twenty or thirty men, of both factions, would volunteer their labour, and refuse, not only pecuniary recompense, but refreshment even: the fight was suffered to go on; and the breakers of heads were leniently dealt with. These days, I believe, are passed, or fast passing; but there is still far too little energy shewn in putting down faction. It is true, that in many remote places — and it is often in the remotest spots that these encounters take place — there are no military, and few policemen; but a resident magistrate, if he be a man fit for his office, may always be previously informed upon these matters. He knows that a faction exists in his neighbourhood; he knows that the fair is drawing near; he knows, that at every fair, a fight takes place; and where any agreement has been made to fight out the quarrel at the fair, he may, without any difficulty, obtain the most accurate information; and every one knows how easily a mob, especially an Irish mob, is reduced to obedience by a very trifling display of firmness and force. I look upon it as most essential to the prosperity of Ireland, that these factions should be put down. They are nearly as inimical to the investment of capital, and nearly as much encouragers of absenteeism, as many of those other kinds of agitation, which are more familiar to us: and I will again take the liberty of repeating my belief, that the substitution of a stipendiary, for an unpaid magistracy, is essential to the peace of Ireland. It is quite unreasonable to expect that an unpaid magistracy, situated as that magistracy is in Ireland, should do their duty. But, to return to the Ennis assizes.

The most numerous class of cases (with one exception), and the most important class, as throwing the greatest light on the character and state of the people, were those homicides of which I have spoken. The exception in point of number of cases, is rape: of these cases, I think nearly forty were entered for trial: but only a very few of that number were heard; and all of them terminated in acquittal. In nine cases out of ten, the crime is sworn to, merely for the purpose of getting a husband; and the plan generally succeeds. The parties are married before the cause is called for trial; and I have myself seen an earnest negotiation carried on under the piazzas of the court-house, a little while before a case was called. There was the "boy" indicted for a capital crime, but out on bail, as he generally is; and the girl, about to swear away a man's life; and the attorneys, and a large circle of relations, all trying to bring about a marriage, before Pat should be called upon to appear, and answer to the indictment that he, "not having the fear of God before his eyes, and being instigated by the devil," did so and so. In the case to which I was a listener, Pat and the fair one could not agree: the trial went on; and Pat was acquitted.

The number, and nature of these cases, certainly indicate no very high state of morals; for in every one of them, circumstances have occurred, which afford to the prosecutrix *some* ground of charge; and the amicable termination of these cases, shews how small the ground of the *capital* charge is. In these cases too, the want of veracity is strongly displayed; and it certainly impresses a stranger with no very favourable idea of female character, to find a girl falsely swearing a capital charge against a man whom she is willing at that moment to marry.

I saw tried, one of those singular cases of abduction, which very frequently occur in Ireland; and which also throw considerable light on the state of society among the lower ranks. Sham cases of abduction are frequent. The "boy" and the girl are agreed; but the girl's relations being dissentient, owing to her being an heiress, and entitled to a better match, it is made up between the young people, that the girl shall be carried away by apparent force. The youth makes known the case to his friends, and collects a number of associates: they come during the night to the house of the girl, force open the door, seize upon the maid, who, though "nothing loth," screams and makes all the opposition in her power, place her on horseback, and, after escorting her a sufficient distance, deliver her over to the "boy," on whose account the abduction was got up. The charge of abduction which I saw tried at Ennis, was a real abduction however, and a very shameless one, attended with circumstances of great cruelty; and originating, as indeed they always do, in love of money. These abductions are most detrimental to the peace of the country; because a feud is instantly generated, between the relatives of the girl, and those of the aggressor; and many subsequent fights invariably result from these outrages.

One of the cases tried at the Ennis assizes, was in many respects similar to that celebrated case, which was the foundation of that excellent novel, "The Collegians." A man was tried for the murder of a girl whom he had seduced; he killed her, and buried her in a peat-rick; and the similarity is the stronger, inasmuch as he was at the time, in treaty to marry another, not so highborn a damsel indeed, as Anne Chute; but high enough and rich enough, to induce him to sacrifice *his* Elie O'Connor. In this case, one of the witnesses, on being desired to identify the prisoner, and being asked the question, "Is that the man?" turned round and recognizing the prisoner, said, "That's him," and added, "How are you Paddy?" nodding familiarly and good-humouredly to the accused. The man was convicted, and hanged.

Another case tried, arose out of one of those disputes, which so frequently originate in the possession of, and competition for, land. It was a case wherein a widow paid an enormous rent for a bit of potato land; and the rent not being paid, and the mischievous power of distraining being resorted to, the possessor endeavoured to save some portion of the potatoes. This gave rise to a fight; and the fight occasioned man-slaughter. In this case, there was much false swearing, and much difficulty in arriving at the truth; and the case strongly impressed upon me the conviction, that the power of distraining, in the hands of the lower orders, is a most mischievous power.

I noticed, that great importance is attached to kissing the book; and sometimes, this ceremony is required, for greater security, to be performed two or three times. Without kissing the book, a witness looks upon his oath as very imperfectly taken; and it is necessary that in the act of kissing, the witness be narrowly watched, lest he kiss his own thumb — with which he holds the book — in place of the book itself.

I noticed also, in the examination of one of the witnesses, a proof of the prevailing belief in the "good people," or fairies. A witness, being asked upon his oath, whether a certain individual could have made his way out of a room, the door and windows of which had been fastened, said, with the utmost gravity, it was impossible he could have got out, unless by enchantment; meaning by this, without the assistance of the good people.

To attend an Irish assize, is certainly not the means by which a stranger is likely to obtain favourable impressions of Irish character. Few of its favourable traits are exhibited there; while all the darker shades are made but too manifest. Want of veracity, on the most solemn occasion on which veracity is ever called for, is but too plainly established. We find the very reverse of that straightforwardness, which it is so delightful to see exhibited in the examination of a witness. If positive falsehood will serve the end, it is unhesitatingly resorted to; and as for telling the *whole* truth, I saw no one instance of it.

But the most striking defect of character which is brought to light, is a perfect contempt of human suffering, and an utter disregard even of the value of human life. Weapons, of the most deadly description, are brought into court as evidence, — sticks and whips loaded with lead; and stones, that might crush the head of a horse. A ruffian may occasionally be found in England, who would slay a man alive to become possessed of his purse; but I greatly question whether out of Ireland, fifty men could be found in any one parish, in any country in Europe, ready to beat one another's brains out with sticks and stones, and all but glorying in the deed. And, as I have already observed, the same ferocity which has been exhibited at the fight, is brought into court: false oaths are the substitutes for weapons: and by these, witnesses seek to avenge the death of a relative who has been more unfortunate, but probably not more criminal, than the accused.

I was much struck at Ennis, as I had been at Tralee, with the acuteness and talent of the Irish attorneys. Their cross-examinations of witnesses were admirable; certainly not surpassed by the very best cross-examinations I ever heard from the mouth of an English barrister.

A day or two before the conclusion of the Clare assizes, I left Ennis for Limerick; returning by a road different from that by which I had gone to Ennis, and through an equally interesting and fertile country.

The Irish Petty Sessions Court

CHAPTER VI.

Limerick, the Shannon, Adair

Return to Limerick — The New and Old Towns — Present State of the Trade of Limerick — Prosperity — Projected Improvements — Mr. Spring Rice — Public Institutions — The Lunatic Asylum — The Barrington Hospital — Antiquities — Condition of the Destitute Poor, and unemployed Artizans of Limerick — Minute Details — Poor laws — a Mont de Pieti — Loan Fund — Environs of Limerick — Lands and Rents — Embarkments on the Shannon — The Village of Adair — Currah, and Dunraven.

I know of no town in which so distinct a line is drawn between its good and its bad quarters, as in Limerick. A person arriving in Limerick by one of the best approaches, and driving to an hotel in George Street, will probably say, "What a very handsome city this is!" while, on the other hand, a person entering the city by the old town, and taking up his quarters there — a thing, indeed, not likely to happen — would infallibly set down Limerick as the very vilest town he had ever entered. The new town of Limerick is, unquestionably, superior to any thing out of Dublin. Its principal street, although less picturesque than the chief streets of Cork, would generally be reckoned a finer street. It is straight, regular, and modern looking; and contains abundance of good private houses and of excellent shops: and although there is less the appearance of business in Limerick than in Cork, and fewer evidences of affluence in its neighbourhood; yet, in the more modern aspect of every thing, there are more certain proofs of improvement than in the former city. The new town of Limerick is, indeed, of recent origin; and the various indications of prosperity which Limerick presents, are all of them true indications.

The advance of the prosperity of Limerick, has been rapid and uniform. The amount of exports has nearly doubled since the year 1822. Nor has this increase been in only one branch of trade. With very few exceptions, it has attended every branch. The corn export trade, especially, has advanced. In 1822, the export of wheat was 102,593 barrels; in 1828, the export had increased to 150,583 barrels; in 1832, the quantity exported was 194,144 barrels; and in 1833, 218,915. In barley, the export has never been great; and although it has doubled since the year 1824, it has somewhat decreased during the last two years. In oats, the increase has been very great. From 155,000 barrels, exported in 1822, the quantity had risen, in 1832, to 408,000. In flour and oatmeal, too, the increase of export has been steady and great. Of the former article, 172 cwt. only was exported in 1824. In 1828, the quantity had risen to upwards of 6000 cwt.; in 1832, it was 33,000 cwt.; and in 1833, upwards of 37,000. In oatmeal, the advance has been equally great. The butter trade, which I have found rather declining in most other places, exhibits no symptom of decline in Limerick. In 1822, 42,869 firkins were exported; in 1831, 67,699 firkins were exported; the following year, there was an advance upon this quantity; and in 1833, 75,000 firkins were exported. In many other articles of trade, the increase has been equally great: but the general increase of trade, is best observed by the estimated value of the whole exports. In 1822, the estimated value was £479,538; in 1830, the estimated value was £720,266 the following year, it was £854,406; in 1832, it was £1,005,945; and in 1833, £936,995. The tonnage of vessels clearing out of the port, exhibits the same advance. In 1822, the tonnage was 29,876; in 1825, 41,871; in 1831, 52,326; in 1833, 56,850.

From these data, I think I may venture to pronounce Limerick to be at this moment an advancing city; and if certain improvements now in contemplation, be carried into effect, there is little reason to doubt, that the progress of Limerick will be even more rapid than it has hitherto been. The improvement to which I particularly allude is, the construction of a dock, by which the great drawback on the trade of Limerick — want of floating depth of water at low tide — will be obviated. The plan proposed, is a bold one: it is, to throw a dam completely across the river, at some distance below the town; so that vessels of 500 or 600 tons will be enabled to come up the river, and find a dock with from 20 to 24 feet of water.

This is not the only improvement that is in progress in Limerick. A handsome new bridge across the Shannon is nearly completed; and a fine square is laid down, railed round, and planted, though not yet built upon. The centre of this square is adorned with a fluted pillar, surmounted by a statue of Mr. Spring Rice, — an honour well merited by that gentleman; — for to his public spiritedness and exertions, the city of Limerick is mainly indebted for every improvement that has either been completed, or that is now in progress.

The public institutions of Limerick are on a fine scale, and some of them, under excellent management. Among the most interesting of these, the Lunatic Asylum may be mentioned. It is, indeed, a pattern for all such institutions. I have never anywhere seen a better example of what may be accomplished by proper management. The building, in its exterior, might be the residence of a nobleman; its interior would put to shame the best scrubbed parlour of Rotterdam; and, in viewing its inmates, madness appears divested of half its horrors. When I visited this institution, it contained 204 persons, only four of whom were that day under coercion.

The county gaol is also reputed to be one of the most approved prisons in the kingdom. I did not visit it; but I believe it is conducted on the same system as the Cork county gaol, of which I have already spoken.

There are several institutions in Limerick, for the alleviation of man's bodily sufferings; and amongst these, I would particularly mention "Barrington's Hospital;" not only because it is one of the best conducted; but also, that I may have an opportunity of mentioning, — as it deserves to be mentioned, — the name of a family to whom the poor of Limerick are so deeply indebted. This hospital was built, and presented to the city, by the family of Sir Joseph Barrington; and as some evidence of the extensive benefit conferred on the city by this institution, I may mention, that no fewer than 14,000 persons were relieved at the dispensary attached to the hospital, during the last six months. Important additions to this hospital are at present contemplated by Mr. M. Barrington, who seems resolved not to stint his beneficence, but is willing rather, that the capabilities of the institution shall keep pace with the wants of the city. Hospitals are frequently endowed with the wealth which the rich cannot carry into the grave with them; but to found an hospital during a man's lifetime, is an act that deserves to be recorded, and remembered.

I visited, in Limerick, an extensive school for females, which is assisted by the new education board. I found about four hundred children, receiving a useful education, — able, in general, to write well; perfectly instructed in reading; and exhibiting, in their appearance and behaviour, the utmost order and neatness. This school is situated in the old town; which contains other objects to interest a stranger. Thomond-bridge is among the most curious of the ancient monuments of Limerick. The irregularity and rude antiquity of its structure, are equally curious to the antiquarian, and striking to the lover of the picturesque. The bridge is supposed to have been built about the year 1210; it is perfectly level, and is built upon fourteen arches.

Another interesting monument, is the cathedral, a large shapeless pile, with a handsome interior; and with a tower, which every stranger ought to ascend; for there is no elevation adjacent to Limerick, from which any satisfactory view of the city can be obtained; and from this tower, not only the city, but a large portion of the counties of Limerick and Clare, is laid open; and the tortuous course of the noble Shannon is made intelligible. Unless there be a considerable eminence contiguous to a town, the readiest way of becoming acquainted with its situation, form, and extent, is to climb the steps of the highest church tower. I never omit to do this.

To the antiquarian, there are many interesting vestiges in the old towns of Limerick. The Limerick reader will understand why I say towns; to the English reader it requires to be told, that there is an English and an Irish town. Remnants of walls, and isolated bastions, are here and there discovered; and the stone, on which the treaty of Limerick was signed, is pointed out to the stranger.

But there are objects of a far different nature, in the old towns of Limerick; — objects of a deeper, and more melancholy interest.

The reader will recollect, that in Cork, Waterford, Kilkenny, and in other towns which I have visited, I have made it a part of my duty to inquire into the condition of the poor; and having been informed by those upon whom I thought some reliance was to be placed, that I should find more and deeper destitution in Limerick, than in any place which I had yet visited, my inquiries in Limerick were prosecuted with all the care which I was capable of bestowing; and I regret to say, that I found too dreadful confirmation of the very worst reports. I spent a day in visiting those parts of the city, where the greatest destitution and misery were said to exist. I entered upwards of forty of the abodes of poverty; and to the latest hour of my existence, I can never forget the scenes of utter and hopeless wretchedness that presented themselves that day. I shall endeavour to convey to the reader some general idea of what I saw.

Some of the abodes I visited were garrets, some were cellars; some were hovels on the ground floor, situated in narrow yards, or alleys. I will not speak of the filth of the places; *that* could not be exceeded in places meant to be its receptacles. Let the worst be imagined, and it will not be beyond the truth. In at least three-fourths of the hovels which I entered, there was no furniture of any description, save an iron pot, — no table, no chair, no bench, no bedstead; — two, three, or four little bundles of straw, with, perhaps, one or two scanty and ragged mats, were rolled up in the corners, unless where these beds were found occupied. The inmates, were some of them old, crooked, and diseased; some younger, but emaciated, and surrounded by starving children; some were sitting on the damp ground, some standing, and many were unable to rise from their little straw heaps. In scarcely one hovel, could I find even a potato. In one which I entered, I noticed a small opening, leading into an inner room. I lighted a bit of paper, at the embers of a turf which lay in the chimney, and looked in. It was a cellar wholly dark; and about twelve feet square: two bundles of straw lay in two corners; on one, sat a bed-ridden woman; on another, lay two naked children, — literally naked, with a torn rag of some kind thrown over them both. But I saw worse even than this. In a cellar which I entered, and which was almost quite dark, and slippery with damp, I found a man sitting on a little sawdust.

He was naked: he had not even a shirt: a filthy and ragged mat was round him: this man was a living skeleton; the bones all but protruded through the skin: he was literally starving.

In place of forty hovels, I might have visited hundreds. In place of seeing, as I did, hundreds of men, women, and children, in the last state of destitution, I might have seen thousands. I entered the alleys, and visited the hovels, and climbed the stairs at a venture; I did not select; and I have no reason to believe that the forty which I visited, were the abodes of greater wretchedness than the hundreds which I passed by.

I saw also, another kind of destitution. The individuals I have yet spoken of, were aged, infirm, or diseased: but there was another class, fast approaching infirmity and disease; but yet able and willing to earn their subsistence. I found many hand-loom weavers, who worked from five in the morning till eight at night, and received from a task-master, from half a crown to four shillings a week. Many of these men had wives and families; and I need scarcely say, that confinement, labour, scanty subsistence, and despair, were fast reducing these men to the condition of the others, upon whom disease, and utter destitution had already laid their hands. The subsistence of these men consisted of one scanty meal of dry potatoes daily.

I will only add one other instance of destitution. Driving in the neighbourhood of Limerick, on the Adair road, in company with a medical gentleman, the apparition of a man suddenly appeared by the side of our car. The gentleman who accompanied me knew him: he had been a stone-breaker; but had become infirm, and at length utterly disabled, by disease, from labour: his cabin was close by; and we ascertained, that he, and his family, had subsisted, during the last three days, on the leaves of that yellow-flowered weed which grows among the corn; and which is boiled, and eaten with a little salt. I think I have already mentioned the use of this weed for a similar purpose, by the destitute poor of Kilkenny; or if I have not, I ought to have done so.

I think it is impossible for me to select a better opportunity than this, to advert briefly to a topic, on which I have not hitherto offered any direct observations. I allude to the disputed question, whether there be, or be not, a necessity for some legal provision for the poor: and I confess, that with such scenes before me as I have at this moment, it does seem to me an insult to humanity and common sense, to doubt the necessity to which I allude. I might carry the reader back with me, to gather arguments from Kilkenny, Waterford, Cashel; and, indeed, from almost every town, village, and hamlet, that has kin on my way; but the situation of the poor of Limerick is at this moment fresh in my memory; and I ask any man of ordinary intelligence, whether such a state of things can, or ought to be allowed to continue? Why should Lord Limerick, in Ireland, be exempt from the duty which Lord Limerick, in England, must perform? Why, under the same government, should men be allowed to starve in one division of the empire, and not in another? I mention the name of Lord Limerick, not because I suppose he, or any other man, can prevent pauperism on his city property; but because, when I inquire who are the individuals that contribute to keep the bodies and souls of these miserable creatures together, and when I ascertain, that many a humane citizen contributes more than the noble owner of all the property, then I perceive, that there is something wrong; and, — that leaving for a moment the question, as it relates to the poor, out of consideration, justice demands, that in the ratio of their abundance, men should be forced to contribute.

At present, I shall not pursue the subject farther. But in a future chapter, when I shall have seen every part of Ireland, I shall speak at greater length, and with more confidence. This I mean to do, with reference to a Poor Law Commission, which was prosecuting its inquiries while I was in Ireland. By the kindness of friends, I was furnished with all the papers which government intended should guide the inquiries of the commissioners: and when I shall have travelled over every part of Ireland, I shall probably feel myself competent to furnish some answer to the queries which are contained in the instructions alluded to; and possibly, to present my own report.

A prospectus for establishing, in this city, a *Mont de Piete,* or charitable pawn-office, fell into my hands. The project originated with Mr. Barrington; and, certainly, from the statements made in the prospectus to which I allude, any substitute for the common pawn-broking system ought to meet with encouragement. The rate of interest, 30 per cent, sanctioned by government, is increased to a ruinous degree, by the necessity of redeeming and repawning weekly, in place of monthly. One shilling lent, and received in the week, pays 1d. interest, and 1d. for the duplicate: this is 8s. 8d. interest on one shilling, for a year; or £8 13s. 4d. on a pound, for a year; or £886. 13s. 4d. per cent., per annum; and this, exclusive of compound interest. The prospectus, after setting forth the wrongs suffered by the necessitous, under the present system, proposes that the profits of the establishment, after paying expenses, shall be applied, in the first instance, in payment of the interest of the capital lent, at 5 per cent., and that the surplus profits shall be divided into equal shares: one, in paying off the debentures; and the other (and when the debentures are paid, the whole) in maintaining and extending the benefits of the hospital. I have dwelt the longer upon this matter, from the belief which I entertain, that the miserable condition of the poor of Ireland is made greatly more miserable, by the extortionate system of common pawn-broking; and that an important relief would be afforded to the poor, by the establishment, wherever practicable, of a *Mont de Piete,* to which the needy man may go with confidence — secure against usurious exaction — knowing that he will receive the fair value on the article deposited; that no advantage will be taken of his ignorance or necessity; and that he is, at the same time, obtaining relief for the present, and contributing to a fund which will comfort and relieve him in the hour of distress. I sincerely trust Mr. Barrington may be successful in his attempt, and that the benefits to the poor of Limerick, which would infallibly follow, may lead to similar institutions elsewhere.

There is in Limerick, as in Cork, and several other places, a loan fund, the residue of subscriptions for the distressed Irish, which was apportioned by the London Committee, in 1822, to different counties, for the promotion of industry. I have a statement, now before me, of the present condition of this fund; and it will surprise the reader to be told, that, while the sum put at the disposal of the county of Limerick has increased, by judicious management, since the year 1822, from £6370 to £7521, and, in other counties, in greater or less proportion, — in some counties it has remained stationary, or suffered a decrease. In Clare, the £6000 intended to be applied to the benefit of the industrious, by loan, at a small interest, and on proper security, has become £5989. In Sligo, the £3870 has become £3831. In Leitrim there has been on the original £2000, a decrease of no less than £867; and perhaps the most singular fact of all is, that the £2500 allocated to Tipperary is, at this moment, precisely £2500. There must have been somewhere gross mismanagement, or grosser jobbing. Where has the £2500 been since 1822? It can never have been applied as intended, because a single loan made, must have either added to, or taken from it; it cannot have lain in a bank, because interest would have accrued upon it! From all that I could ascertain, both in Cork and in Limerick, I have reason to think that this loan fund has been most beneficial in its effects; and that any loan fund, under judicious management, must produce important results, in encouraging industry, and accumulating capital.

I have said nothing, as yet, of the environs of Limerick. In the neighbourhood of such a river as the Shannon, they can scarcely be otherwise than beautiful; and the great natural fertility of the soil, and the improved husbandry, pretty generally adopted, greatly increase the attractions of this fine district. The Marquis of Lansdowne possesses an extensive estate close to Limerick. It is in the finest state of cultivation; and, from a personal survey, I may state that every industrious tenant is in comfortable circumstances; and that the moderate rent charged for the excellent land in this neighbourhood, was in striking contrast with the rents paid for the comparatively indifferent land which I had lately seen in the neighbourhood of Ennis.

I cannot speak so well of the property of the Earl of Limerick. Whatever advantages the tenantry possess, are referable to the exertions and good-heartedness of his lordship's agents. I will not trust myself to speak further of the Earl of Limerick, unless only to add, that from high and low, rich and poor, I never heard a good word of his lordship.

Some extensive embankments are now in course of being constructed below Limerick, with the view of reclaiming land. One of these, the lowest down the river, is undertaken by a Scotch gentleman, who has already sunk a large sum in the attempt: the others are undertaken by Lord Lansdowne and by Mr. Barrington; and there is no doubt of the ultimate success of all these attempts. Before leaving Limerick, I visited the beautiful village of Adair, and the fine domains of the Earl of Dunraven, and of Sir Aubrey de Vere.

This was one of the most agreeable days I have spent. I took a circuitous road, skirting the left bank of the Shannon, and visiting a village, called Palace, on my way, that I might have the pleasure of looking in upon the talented author of "The Collegians." Carragh, the domain of Sir Aubrey de Vere, I greatly admire. Sir Aubrey being then engaged as foreman of the grand jury at Limerick, I had not an opportunity of presenting my letter of introduction. It is only when I do not, or have not an opportunity of presenting my letters of introduction, that I mention them at all; and this, not as information to the public, to whom the matter is of no importance; but for the information of the individuals who gave me the letters, and of the individuals to whom they were addressed, who may possibly be aware of my having been in possession of such letters; and who, without some mention of them, would be ignorant of the reason why they were not used.

Adair, and the domain of the Earl of Dunraven (to whom I also carried a letter, which I did not deliver), are both beautiful. Within Lord Dunraven's domain are no fewer than three ruins of abbeys, — one of them, the Black Abbey, yet in tolerable preservation. There is also, close to the picturesque bridge over the Maize, the ruins of the castle of the Earls of Desmond. The Earl of Dunraven is now building a new castellated mansion, close to the old house: with Kingston Castle in my recollection, it appeared rather diminutive; but the surrounding scenery is close scenery, and not suitable to a very commanding edifice.

Limerick City, circa 1845

CHAPTER VII.

The Shannon, Portumna,

I now return to the Shannon; from which, the city of Limerick, and its attractions, and interests, have some time diverted me.

It is impossible to ascend by water, from Limerick to the village of Castle Connell, owing to the rapids which intervene: but the road, although not running close to the river, commands its banks; and carries the traveller through as lovely a country as the imagination can well picture. In variety, and wooded fertility, it is not surpassed by the most celebrated of the English vales, no one of which can boast as an adjunct to its scenery, so noble a river as the Shannon. Many fine seats lie on the left of the road, towards the river, particularly Mount Shannon, the residence, at least the property of the Earl of Clare; and glimpses are also caught of several other fine domains and villas, amongst others, those belonging to the numerous family of Massey.

On reaching the village of Castle Connell, my first feeling was admiration; my next, surprise, that I should never before have heard of Castle Connell. It is surrounded by every kind of beauty; and after spending a day in its neighbourhood, I began to entertain serious doubts, whether even Killarney itself greatly surpassed in beauty the scenery around Castle Connell. It is a little village of neat, clean, country houses, situated close to the Shannon, and backed and flanked by noble domains, and fine spreading woods. Just below the village, commence the rapids of the Shannon, of which I had never even heard, until I reached Limerick; and these are of themselves well worth a visit. I hired a little boat to shoot the upper rapid, and take me across; for the scenery is best seen from the Clare side; and I was well repaid for my trouble. A charming walk leads down the opposite bank, through Sir Hugh Massey's grounds; and I do not at this moment recollect any example of more attractive river scenery. The wide, deep, clear river is, for more than a quarter of a mile, almost a cataract; and this, to an English eye, must be particularly striking. It is only in the streams and rivulets of England, that rapids are found: the larger rivers, generally glide smoothly on without impediments from rocks: the Thames, Trent, Mersey, and Severn, when they lose the character of streams, and become rivers, hold a noiseless course; but the Shannon, larger than all the four, here pours that immense body of water, which above the rapids is forty feet deep, and three hundred yards wide, through and above a congregation of huge stones and rocks, which extend nearly half a mile; and offers not only an unusual scene, but a spectacle approaching much nearer to the sublime, than any moderate-sized stream can offer even in its highest cascade. None of the Welsh water-falls, nor the Geisbach in Switzerland, can compare for a moment in grandeur and effect with the rapids of the Shannon.

Nor is the river the only attractive object at Castle Connell: its adjuncts are all beautiful. The greenest of lawns rise from it; the finest timber fringes it: magnificent mansions tower above their surrounding woods; swelling knolls are dotted with cattle and sheep: and it so happened, too, that the landscape had all the advantage which the alternations of sunshine and shadow could give it.

I went as far as a holy well, dedicated to St. Senanus. Judging from what I saw, it must be in high repute; for hundreds of little wooden vessels lay heaped in and above it, the offerings of those who had come to drink; and the trees that overshadowed the well were entirely covered with shreds of all colours — bits and clippings of gowns, and handkerchiefs, and petticoats, — remembrances also of those who drank. These, I believe, are the title-deeds to certain exemptions, or benefits, claimed by those who thus deposit them in the keeping of the patron saint, who is supposed to be thus reminded of the individuals whose penances might otherwise have been overlooked. I noticed among the offerings, some strings of beads, and a few locks of hair.

The inn at Castle Council is beautifully situated, and very moderate in its charges; and the inhabitants of Limerick make abundant use of it: for, besides that Castle Connell is resorted to as summer quarters, it is also a noted rendezvous of the tradespeople, on Sundays and holidays. Houses are scarce and dear. For a very small house, £10 a month is asked; and a couple of rooms indifferently furnished, could not be had for less than 25s. per week. I found this to be universally the case throughout Ireland at all places of occasional resort; everywhere affording proof of want of enterprise in the employment of capital, however judicious the investment might be.

I hired a small rowing boat to take me up the river to Killaloe, where the steam navigation of the upper Shannon commences. The rapids of Castle Connell, although they interrupt the river navigation, are not allowed to impede the water communication between the upper Shannon and Limerick, — a canal being cut from the city, to a point in the Shannon, about a mile and a half above Castle Connell.

Leaving Castle Connell, Clare is on one side, and Limerick county on the other side of the river; but the division line between Limerick and Tipperary is soon passed; and then Clare is on the west, and Tipperary on the east side of the river. Nothing could be greener than the sloping banks which we rowed swiftly by; they were adorned too, on the Limerick side especially, by several pretty villas; and this being hay season, the slanting sunshine, falling athwart the after-grass, bathed it in hues that were almost too brilliant to be natural. The river is here, from two to three hundred yards wide, and averages from thirty to forty feet in depth.

About two miles up the river from Castle Connell we reached O'Brien's bridge; an old bridge, with a castle, and small village, on the Clare side of the river. The bridge has thirteen arches, and is only interesting from its antiquity. There is a slight fall of water; but not so much as to occasion any difficulty or danger, either in ascending, or in shooting the arch. Beyond O'Brien's bridge, the country improves; fine cultivated hills appear at some little distance from the river; and although a deficiency of wood may be remarked, the views on either side present many sweet pictures of quiet pastoral scenery — verdant slopes, and drowsy cattle, and nodding water lilies, and here and there, a farm-house, and its more animated accompaniments. We also passed several small islands, none of them large enough to be made subservient to utility.

About a mile and a half before reaching Killaloe, another canal cut is requisite, owing to some inconsiderable rapids. The canal skirts the domain of the Lord Bishop of Killaloe; whose palace and grounds are sufficiently inviting: the fine long meadow-grass of the bishop's lawn, reminded me by contrast, of a saying I had heard of the county of Kerry, where grass is so scarce, that it is said, the cows wont lift up their heads to look at a passer-by, for fear that they should not be able to find the grass again. I reached Killaloe about four hours after leaving Castle Council.

Killaloe, I found an improving town. This improvement arises from several causes; but chiefly is owing to the spirited proceedings of the Inland Steam Navigation Company, — a company, whose objects are most closely connected with the improvement of Ireland, and which are too important, and too vast, to be left, in the present infancy of the establishment, to private exertion, or even to public patronage. The improvement of the navigation of the Shannon and its tributaries, is deserving of the especial protection and aid of government. Killaloe is the head-quarters of the company; and from this point, there is a regular steam communication for goods and passengers up the Shannon, through Loch Derg, to Portumna, Banagher, and Athlone; and from the same point, by packet boat to Limerick, and thence, again, by steam to the sea. It is intended to carry the steam navigation above Athlone, through Loch Ree, to Lanesborough, Carrick, and Leitrim; and when these arrangements are completed, there will be a direct navigation on the Shannon, of nearly *two hundred and fifty miles,* mostly performed by steam; together with a direct water communication to Dublin, by the grand canal.

I have ascribed the improving condition of Killaloe, chiefly to the enterprise of the steam navigation company. This arises in several ways, — partly in the direct employment afforded by the company in the construction of buildings, docks, &c.; and partly in the general encouragement offered to trade, by the facilities afforded, both for internal communication, and for export trade, which has lately been greatly on the increase. There are also other sources of employment and wealth in Killaloe. The extensive slate quarries in the neighbourhood, afford a yearly export of at least 100,000 tons; and dispense about £300 weekly, in wages: and close to the town, an extensive mill has lately been erected, for the sawing of marble and stone, which are sent there both from Galway and Limerick counties: so that altogether there is little want of employment in Killaloe.

The town is very agreeably situated on the rising ground above the river, and within a mile of the noble expansion of water, called Loch Derg. An old bridge of nineteen arches, just below the town, connects the counties of Clare and Tipperary; and there is an old cathedral, with a square tower, and Saxon archway of considerable beauty. I attempted to gain the summit of the tower, by the stair inside; but found it in so ruinous and dangerous a condition, that I was forced to give up the attempt.

I stepped on board the steam vessel at eight in the morning, satisfied with every thing about Killaloe, excepting the inn, which is far from being what might be expected at the place where the navigation company has fixed its head-quarters. About a mile and a half from Killaloe, just at the entrance to Loch Derg, is a mount on the left bank, covered with trees, called O'Brien's fort, . where it is said, the ancient kings once resided. On entering Loch Derg, several pretty and interesting objects attract one on both sides. The vessel kept nearly mid-water, and this first reach of the loch being only about a mile wide, there is nothing lost to the eye. Derry Castle, the residence of Captain Head, on the Tipperary side, is a beautiful spot: the lawn slopes down to the water; the house is almost hidden in fine woods; and there is a fine back-ground of cultivated mountains. On a little island, close to the shore, are seen the ruins of a castle.

All the way through this first reach of the loch, a distance of about four miles, the character of the banks continues the same: not that there is any thing like monotony; all the variety that can be produced by verdure, wood, and tillage is there: but the banks are invariably sloping and cultivated, with higher and more sterile elevations rising behind; ten or twelve islands, of inconsiderable size, lie scattered over this first reach. At the point where this first reach of the loch terminates, opening into the wider part of the lake, the banks on both sides are extremely beautiful. The Clare side is covered with deep woods, backed by lofty hills; and the Tipperary side is adorned by the fine domain of Castle-loch, embosomed in magnificent oak woods: here, too, an island surmounted by a ruin, is seen on the right, close to the shore; and a small harbour has been constructed in a little bay, for the convenience of the export of slate. This first reach of the loch, varies in depth from thirty up to ninety feet; but in the mid channel, the average depth is from seventy to eighty feet. Close to the shore, there is generally from ten to fifteen feet water; and at some parts, as much as forty feet.

Immediately, on emerging from the first reach, the loch spreads both to the left and right. The left reach, which is not the path of the vessel, is an interesting one. Clare is on one side of it, and county Galway on the other. On the Clare side, the nearer banks are finely cultivated and well wooded; and more than one ruined castle is seen rising from the water's edge. One of these castles was some time ago held in forcible possession by illicit distillers, against all the civil force that attempted, from time to time, to dislodge them: and it was at length found necessary, to batter down the sheltering walls with cannon ball. On the Galway side, the scenery is diversified by several fine country seats, and by the prettily situated village, called Mount Shannon. Several islands, also, adorn this reach; particularly Holy island, — covered with beautiful green pasturage, on which there is an extensive grazing; and where also, is one of the ancient round towers, besides some lesser and more imperfect ruins. The other islands are no way remarkable. With the exception of Bushy island, which is what it professes to be, they are destitute of wood.

Leaving this reach of which I have just been speaking, to the left, we now turned into the main reach of the loch. The banks are now, for a few miles, less interesting on the Tipperary side; but on the Galway shore, several gentlemen's seats are seen, and a tolerable sprinkling of wood. We made a short halt at a place, formerly called Cow island, now christened Williamstown. Here an hotel is in course of being built; and it is in contemplation to make this a point of export from the county of Clare, and to construct a road to Ennis, its chief town. Opposite to this, on the Tipperary side, many interesting objects are descried: several old castles frown on the shores of two deep bays, Youghal and Dromineer bay, which diverge far to the right; and here and there, more modern houses, with sweeping lawns, and crowning woods, give animation to the scene.

The slow rate at which the steamer carried us through the lake, afforded ample time for observation; and although the weather was not what would generally be called fine, and gave rise to much grumbling among the passengers, I was not among the number of grumblers. It was not, indeed, one of those splendid summer days, when lakes are like mirrors, and woods are mirrored in them; when the green slopes seem to bask in sunshine, and repose dwells among the hills. It was all sorts of weather: we had gleams of sunshine; sudden mists; flying showers; moments of calm; sweeping breezes: so that in the course of one voyage up Loch Derg, I had the advantage of seeing it under as many aspects, as if I had traversed it in every season.

After passing Cow island, the loch bends a little to the left; and just at the bend, we passed close to a large island called Flanmore, — a green sloping island, on which I noticed some ruins. On the Galway side, the country here is wild and uninteresting; but on the Tipperary shore, villas are scattered here and there; and as we proceeded farther, they became more numerous. The lake here, for several miles, is not more than a mile in width; and the Tipperary banks are as full of beauty, as wood, lawn, cultivation, and villas, can make them. The domain of Castle Biggs, is particularly attractive. A fine swelling headland projects into the lake; a grey stern ruin stands close to the water; while the modern house, in the midst of a beautiful park, looks down upon a pretty cove, studded with green islands. Opposite to this, on the Galway side, the banks are thickly covered with wood, which is not, however of large growth; and a wild uninteresting tract of country reaches along Cloongagave bay, — the last into which the loch expands on the left.

We were now within sight of Portumna town and Portumna lodge, — or rather, the remains of what was once the fine seat of the Marquis of Clanricarde. Its situation is not particularly happy: the country is flat, and the wood generally of small growth; and it is not believed that the Marquis will ever again rebuild his mansion.

The great reach of Loch Derg, through which I have just conducted the reader, contains upwards of forty islands, varying in size from a mere point, to the circumference of perhaps two English miles. The loch, not reckoning in its width, the great reach which has Clare on one side, and Galway on the other, is from one to three miles broad. The depth is very variable. There is, however, everywhere, a sufficiency of water for all the purposes of navigation. The length of this expansion of the Shannon, *from Port*umna to Killaloe, is twenty-three miles.

The town of Portumna lies about a quarter of a mile from the river, and I had only time for a flying visit; for I wished to take advantage of the fine evening, and go forward to Banagher, in the small river steamer, to which the passengers from Killaloe are transferred. Portumna is a place of considerable export trade to Dublin, and enjoys a good retail trade besides; but the improvement of the town is much checked by the disinclination of the Marquis of Clanricarde to grant good leases.

The distance up the river, from Portumna to Banagher, is fourteen miles and a half; and, by the bye, I must not omit to note the expense of travelling by steam on the Shannon. The distance from Killaloe to Banagher, is thirty-eight miles; and for this, the charge is 6s. 4d., or 2d. per mile. The charge is certainly not high; and I understood that the only ground of complaint — the slow rate of travelling — was on the eve of being removed, by the employment of a new steam vessel of greater power. The company has already done wonders; and it would be absurd, as yet, to expect perfection. To the lover of the picturesque, the banks of the Shannon, between Portumna and Banagher, present little that is attractive. But to other minds, there may be an interest of perhaps a higher kind. We are navigating in a steam vessel, a river, here a hundred and thirty miles from the sea; and we know it to be navigable nearly a hundred miles higher. Its volume appears to be as great as when we saw it at Limerick: it is several hundred yards broad; and twenty and thirty feet deep. What a body of water is this! What are the Thames, the Medway, the Mersey, the Severn, the Trent, the Humber, the Tweed, or the Clyde, a hundred and thirty miles from the sea? I am not sure if they exist at all; or if any of them do, they are but brawling streams for the minnow to sport in. There is, in fact, an approach to the sublime, in the spectacle of such a river as this; and the feeling receives aid from the character of its banks. These are wide, and apparently interminable plains, unenclosed, — almost level with the river, — bearing luxuriant crops of herbage, and feeding innumerable herds. We see scarcely any habitations: no villages or hamlets; and no road or traffic on the banks. The meadows of which I speak, extend on both sides of the river, the greater part of its course from Banagher to Portumna. These meadows are all overflowed during the winter, and are let for grazing at a very high rent. For many miles, there is nothing to relieve the monotony of these vast flats, excepting an old castle, called Torr Castle, — not otherwise remarkable than as being the only object which breaks the level. The views on this part of the Shannon, brought forcibly to my recollection, the banks of the Guadalquiver, between Seville and Cadiz.

Six or seven miles above Portumna, the river branches out, leaving several flat green islands; on one of which a Martello tower, once a defence against the people of Connaught, is still foolishly kept up. The ruins of Meeleck monastery, too, on the Galway side, attract the attention. They appeared to be both fine and extensive. It is here, that the lower Brusna river falls into the Shannon. It is the boundary line betwixt the provinces of Leinster and Munster; and is one of those aids, which may be brought to bear advantageously on the Shannon navigation. From the point of junction, it is only eight miles to the town of Birr, and at a very moderate expense, the Brusna may be rendered navigable.

From this point to Banagher, the river flows in various branches, leaving not fewer than twenty islands, great and small. The country on both sides, too, begins to improve; and to assume greater variety. Wood, though but of scanty growth, begins to appear, and the ground rises into some considerable elevations. I reached Banagher a little before dusk, and found excellent accommodation in the only hotel. This town, like all the others on the line of the inland navigation, is progressively advancing. There is a good corn market, a considerable export, and a thriving retail trade. The town itself has little in its appearance to recommend it. It consists chiefly of one very long street; and has some batteries on the Connaught side; and a bridge of nineteen arches.

To have had the advantage of a steam vessel from Banagher up the river to Athlone, I should have been obliged to have remained at Banagher several days; for, at present, this convenience occurs only twice a week. I sufficiently ascertained, however, that by travelling to Athlone by land, I should lose little in the attractions of scenery. The river, from Athlone to Banagher, flows through a wide tract of bog land, — even more uninteresting than the meadows which extend between Portumna and Banagher. The only relief from this monotony, is the Seven Churches, — ruins, which stand close by the river, about ten miles above Banagher.

I hired a car to Athlone, and left Banagher the day after I arrived in it. Here I found a change in the expense of travelling. Posting by car, had hitherto been everywhere 8d. per mile; but I now found, that the price varied with the number of persons using the car. If one person only travels, the price is 6d. per mile; if two travel, it is 8d.; if three travel, it is 10d.

For some miles after leaving Banagher, the road keeps near to the river; and then passes through the station, called Shannon Harbour, where the Grand Canal to Dublin connects itself with the Shannon. From this point, there is a regular communication daily; both to Dublin, and, by steam, on the Shannon to Limerick. A little beyond Shannon harbour, we crossed the upper Brusna river, at a point where the wood scenery is extremely beautiful, and where also, the fine domain of Colonel L'Estrange skirts the road.

Soon after, we entered that wide tract of bog land, which I have described the Shannon as traversing. It extended on both sides of the road, as far as the eye could reach; and presented, under the influence too, of a dull atmosphere, as dreary a prospect as can well be conceived. The Bog of Allan, which traverses a great part of King's County, lay on our right: and the bogs of Galway stretched away to the left. Occasionally, as the road ascended some trifling elevation., the Shannon was discovered, winding its brimful course, through the low, wide, brown, bog lands, which extended far on either side of it. To the utilitarian, even this prospect is not deficient in interest. Turf — that article of prime necessity in Ireland — is not equally abundant in all parts; and here, in the extensive bogs through which a great river flows, there is security for an abundant and cheap supply of fuel to parts the most remote.

The road between Banagher and Athlone, I found one of the worst I had seen in Ireland. Few gentlemen's seats are in its neighbourhood; and therefore, it is nobody's interest to make a job. Some considerable distance before reaching Athlone the country improves, and the immediate neighbourhood of the town is finely diversified and well cultivated.

CHAPTER VIII.

Athlone

Athlone — The Bridge and the Shannon — Barracks and Fortifications — Ballymahon — Land, Landlords, and Rents in the County of Longford — Condition of the Farmers — The Protestant Population — Religious Dissention — Want of Sympathy with the People, on the part of the Aristocracy — Labouring Classes — Con-acre — Irish Opposition to the Law — The Protestant Clergy — The Catholic Priesthood — Trading Magistrates — Necessity for a Stipendiary Magistracy.

Athlone is a remarkably ugly town. So deficient is it in good streets, that after I had walked over the whole town, I still imagined I had seen only the suburbs. But it is, notwithstanding, both an interesting town, and an excellent business town. It stands in the midst of a well cultivated and thickly peopled country; and, both in its export and general trade, is rapidly improving. At least eighty tons, chiefly corn, are sent down the Shannon, on a weekly average, by the Navigation Company. The bridge is extremely ancient, and is in a disgracefully ruinous condition. In many places the parapet wall has given way; and the carriage road is so narrow that, on a market-day, it frequently happens that one can pass in no other manner than by jumping from cart to car and from car to cart. The bridge is altogether a disgrace to the town and the kingdom. Notwithstanding that between Athlone and Portumna, the Shannon receives the two Brusna rivers, the Suck, and many smaller tributaries, it appears at Athlone, to carry an undiminished volume of water. Above Athlone bridge — upwards of a hundred and fifty miles from the sea — the river is three hundred yards wide, and ranges from twenty to thirty-five feet in depth.

Athlone is a great military station. Extensive barracks, both for foot regiments and for artillery, lie in its immediate neighbourhood; and, on the Connaught side, a line of fortifications has been erected. In the very centre of the town, too, there is an ancient castle, with a strong central tower, and massive bastions. All these places are fully garrisoned.

Athlone, I made my head-quarters for a week; and, from it, made excursions through different parts of the county of Longford. Independently of my chief objects of inquiry, another object of interest presented itself, in the reputed birth-place of Goldsmith, and in the scene of "The Deserted Village," to both of which I shall by and by return.

Ballymahon was one of my central points. This is a town about ten miles from Athlone, and capable of much improvement. A very fertile country surrounds it: it is sufficiently near to water communication; and some idea may be formed of the extent of its market, when I mention that from £300 to £400 worth of eggs have been sold on one market-day. The town and its capabilities are, however, utterly neglected by the proprietor, who grants no leases, and acts — as a great majority of landlords do — as if he had no interest in the permanent improvement of his property.

Land, throughout the county of Longford, is, with few exceptions, let high, but there *are* exceptions. Lady Ross forms one of these. The land on her ladyship's estate is well worth the value put upon it, and, with a little more skill and industry, would afford even higher rents than are exacted. But there is a lamentable want of good husbandry; clean farming appears to be unknown: everywhere fields are seen covered with luxuriant crops of weeds, to be ploughed in as manure; and nowhere is there visible any of the neatness and care which are indicative of industrious habits. I visited a farmer who possessed 107 acres at 23s. the Irish acre (not above 16s. the English acre), almost every acre of the farm arable; and yet this man had as few comforts about him as are found among the holders of a few acres. It must not be forgotten, however, that one would frequently judge erroneously of the condition of a farmer, by observing only his way of life. More minute observation and closer inquiries must be made. Comfort, as we understand it, is neither understood nor relished in Ireland. I know examples, both in this and in other counties, of persons, living in the most miserable way, leaving considerable sums behind them; and giving handsome portions to their daughters. I do not adduce these examples with the view of insinuating that the land-occupiers are in a better condition than they appear to be. If examples occasionally occur, of farmers leaving behind them old stockings, full of sovereigns, or of portioning off their daughters handsomely, this is accomplished at the expense of all that we should call the necessaries of life; and I cannot think it any brilliant example of prosperity, that a farmer should leave a bag of gold behind him, if he and his family have subsisted all their lives on dry potatoes. To entitle one to say that a farmer can live out of his land, he must be able to pay his rent; to live comfortably; to educate and provide for his family; and to do something towards improving his land. I fear, however, if such were the standard by which the condition of the Irish land-occupiers were to be judged, we should be brought to the conclusion, that none of the landholders in Ireland, excepting perpetual leaseholders, can live out of their land.

There is a considerable Protestant population in the county of Longford; but I was sorry to learn that much bad feeling existed, owing to a difference in religious belief. A trifling example of this occurred while I was in the neighbourhood. Lady Ross had established several Protestant schools: and the Catholic children of the adjoining village, were accustomed to post themselves on a bridge, across which the Protestant children were obliged to pass, and to spit upon them as they passed by. Several of these offenders were brought before an active and impartial neighbouring magistrate, who, very properly, sent them to the house of correction. The resident landlords of the county of Longford, are, with few exceptions, an unimproving race; and I regretted to find, that betwixt them and the lower orders, there was not the best understanding. A wealthy and unembarrassed baronet, on being asked, why he did not embellish his domain, which stood greatly in need of it, and thus give some employment to the people, said, "he made it a rule to circumscribe, within the least possible limits, his intercourse with the lower orders." It is not every landlord who might choose so to express himself; but I fear there are too many who so act. I have generally found the landowners extremely ignorant of the real condition of the poor: and how, indeed, are they to gain their knowledge, unless they specially seek it? They do not themselves hire labourers; they do not call on the small farmer for rent; they do not themselves eject or drive for rent; — and it is not to the hall, but to the farm-house, that the mendicant, and the mendicant's wife, and the orphan child, and the unemployed labourer, carry their sack, and their petition. The landlord has his gate-house, beyond which the vigilant porter permits no unwelcome visitor to pass.

The wages of labour throughout the county of Longford are low: 8d. in summer, and 6d. in winter, is the usual rate; and that without diet Many have endeavoured to convince me that this rate is sufficiently high for the quantity of labour performed; and that it would be greater economy to pay 1s. 6d. to an English labourer, than 3d. to an Irishman; and that I might, every hour of the day, have confirmation of this, by observing the listless way a labourer goes about his work. But when I see a labourer leaning on his spade, I do not see, in this, so much a proof of unwillingness to work, as of want of full employment; and I am not aware that there is any complaint of idleness against the migrating Irish, by those who employ them: and besides, — let those who make unfavourable comparisons between English and Irish labourers, ask themselves the question — how an English labourer would work, if a scanty meal of dry potatoes were substituted for bacon and beer?

The con-acre system is universal in this county; and the rent paid does not generally exceed the rate of £8 per acre. The same practice, too, prevails here, as I had found in the county of Kilkenny, and in some other parts, by which the individual furnishing manure receives, rent free, the produce of as much land as he is able to manure. At £7 an acre for manured potato land, the tenant appears to have a good bargain. Add to the £7 - £3 10s. for seed and labour; and suppose the produce of the acre fifteen tons of potatoes, at 2d. per stone. The value would in that case be £20, leaving to the occupier £9 10s. if he sent the potatoes to market. These too, are both low calculations: fifteen tons is not the most abundant produce; and 1d. per stone is a low price. The rent of con-acre here is lower, however, than I have generally found it elsewhere. The reader will recollect that £10 and £12. are the more usual rents.

I regretted to have confirmation in the county of Longford, of that desire generally ascribed to the Irish peasantry, of opposing the course of justice. It has generally been said, that in this, Ireland offers a great contrast to the neighbouring island: that, whereas in England, every man's hand is raised in support of the law; in Ireland, all are arrayed in opposition to it. That there is a considerable degree of truth in this, cannot be denied; though, at the same time, many acts, which, at first sight, might be set down as arising out of pure dislike of the course of justice, appear, upon minuter inquiry to have originated in clanship; and in a conviction common throughout Ireland, of the claim which all relations have to protection, however grievously they may have offended against the law. Examples of this, I think, I have already given, when speaking of the assizes at Ennis. Some facts, however, which came to my knowledge in Longford, were strongly indicative of a determination to set law at defiance; and of a disposition to regard all men as martyrs, or at least as injured persons, who had been brought, by crimes however heinous, within the operation of the law.

I will adduce two instances. A stranger to that part of Ireland, and a Protestant, was servant in the house of a magistrate; and he robbed his master to a considerable extent. This man, though a perfect stranger, was screened by the peasantry during a long period, and was received and entertained on no other passport, than as being in danger of being overtaken by justice for having robbed a good master — a magistrate. Another example is still more striking. An individual, moving in the upper ranks of life, named Luke Dillon, was tried some years ago for rape committed under most aggravated circumstances, the object of the crime, too, being in his own sphere of life. Sentence of death was commuted to banishment for life; and Luke Dillon appeared to be forgotten. A man, however, one day appeared in this neighbourhood, and gave out that *he* was Luke Dillon, returned from banishment, and setting the law at defiance. The man was a swindler, — not Luke Dillon; but he judged — and he judged correctly — that by pretending to be this individual who had suffered under a sentence of the law, and who wished to set it at defiance, he should receive protection, and be enabled the easier to exercise his swindling propensities. This man was apprehended, and brought to trial at the sessions; and it appeared in evidence, that he had been concealed, protected and entertained, as being the infamous wretch who had been banished, and who, it was believed, had been adroit enough to outwit the law.

I was happy to find the Protestant clergy of this part of Ireland greatly respected; and this respect is evinced in singular ways. From time to time, considerable emigration has taken place from this part of Ireland to America; and it is not unusual for remittances to be sent home from the colonies, by those who have emigrated, for the use of their poor relatives. Now it is a curious fact, and a fact that consists with my knowledge, that Catholic emigrants send their remittances to the care, not of the Catholic priest, but of the Protestant clergyman, to be distributed by him among those pointed out. The same respect for, and reliance on, the Protestant clergyman, is evinced in other ways. It is not at all unusual, for Catholics possessed of a little money, to leave the Protestant clergyman their executor, in preference to their own priest, or to any other individual. The Irish peasant has naturally a respect for, and confidence in, a gentleman, of whatever persuasion he is. Ah! how the gentlemen of Ireland have laboured to eradicate this respect, and to destroy this confidence! Yet it still exists; and needs but a little intercourse, and a little kindliness, to be at any time restored.

The influence of the Catholic priesthood is seen on all occasions excepting those in which the guardianship of money is concerned; and it is to be regretted, that this influence is not always well exerted. Every one who knows anything of magisterial business in Ireland, or who has had opportunities of attending assizes or sessions, well knows that this influence is frequently exerted in cooperation with the peasantry against the law; and in screening criminals from its operation. A hundred instances of this are on record. I know a case in the county of Longford, of a man being put upon his trial for abduction, — when the priest volunteered to give the man a character; and yet, the individual tried, had been concerned in two other cases of abduction: and it came out on a cross examination, that these facts were perfectly known to the volunteering priest.

I do look upon it as most important to the civilization and to the peace of Ireland, that a better order of Catholic priesthood should be raised. Taken, as they at present are, from the very inferior classes, they go to Maynooth, and are reared in monkish ignorance and bigotry; and they go to their cures, with a narrow education, grafted on the original prejudices and habits of thinking, which belong to the class among which their early years were passed. From my considerable experience of Catholic countries, I know enough of Popery to convince me how necessary it is, that its priests should have all the advantages which are to be gathered beyond the confines of a cloister.

I found in one part of this county, great want of accommodation for the Protestant congregation. I allude to the parish "of the Union of Kilglass." There is monstrous abuse here. The bishop is rector, and draws from four to five hundred pounds per annum; and yet there is no church, or Protestant service in the parish. His lordship, on being respectfully written to on the subject, replied, that there was service in the next parish!

Trading magistrates are not yet extinct in the county Longford: value is still occasionally received for magisterial protection, in the shape of labour, — such as a winter cutting of turf being brought to a man's door. Neither is there much co-operation among the magistracy. They take pleasure in thwarting each other; and it is not unusual for persons imprisoned by the warrant of one magistrate, to be forthwith liberated by the warrant of another. This, I think, ought not to be possible. Crime can never be effectually repressed, where such a state of things exists; and every week's new experience in Ireland, more and more convinced me, that the establishment of a general stipendiary magistracy, would be one great step towards the civilization and pacification of the country. Without this, the factions which disturb so many of the counties, cannot be put effectually down. The unpaid magistracy of Ireland cannot as a body, practise that steady, fearless, and energetic vindication of the law, which must certainly go hand in hand with every measure of equity and conciliation.

END OF VOL. I.

London:

Printed By Manning And Smithson,   Ivy-lane, Paternoster-row.

Index

Books in the Clachan 'Historic Irish Journeys' series

Travels In Ireland - J.G. Kohl
This is a very readable account by a German visitor of his tour around Ireland immediately before the Great Famine.

Disturbed Ireland – 1881 - Bernard Becker
A series of letters written as the author travelled around the West of Ireland, visiting key places in the 'Land War'. We meet Captain Boycott and other members of the gentry, as well as a range of small farmers and peasants.

A Journey throughout Ireland, During the Spring, Summer and Autumn of 1834, - Henry D. Inglis
Inglis travels Ireland attempting to answer the question, 'is Ireland and improving country?' using discussion with landlords, manufacturers and tenants plus his own insightful observations.

The West Of Ireland: Its Existing Condition and Prospects - Henry Coulter
This is a collection of letters from Saunders's News-Letter relating to the condition and prospects of the people of the West of Ireland after the partial failure of the harvests of the early 1860s.

Also in the 'Local History' Series
Henry Coulter's account has been sub-divided for the convenience of local and family historians

The West Of Ireland: Its Existing Condition and Prospects, Part 1, by Henry Coulter
This is an extract from the complete edition dealing with Athlone, Co. Clare and Co. Galway.

The West Of Ireland: Its Existing Condition and Prospects, Part 2, by Henry Coulter
This is an extract from the complete edition dealing with Co. Mayo.

The West Of Ireland: Its Existing Condition and Prospects, Part 3, by Henry Coulter
The final extract from the complete edition dealing with Counties Co Sligo, Donegal, Leitrim and Roscommon.

J.G.Kohl's account has been sub-divided for the convenience of local and family historians.

Travels in Ireland – Part 1, Takes us through Edgeworthtown, The Shannon, Limerick, Edenvale, Kilrush and Father Mathew.

Travels in Ireland – Part 2, His journey continues through Tarbet, Tralee, Killarney, Bantry, Cork, Kilkenny and Waterford.

Travels in Ireland – Part 3, This section deals with Wexford, Enniscorthy, Avoca, Glendalough and Dublin.

Travels In Ireland - Part 4 – He goes north for the last part of his journey through Dundalk, Newry, Belfast, The Antrim Coast, Rathlin, The Giant's Causeway.

Henry Inglis' book has been sub-divided for the convenience of local and family historians.
**A Journey throughout Ireland, During the Spring, Summer and Autumn of
1834, Vol. 1, Part 1,**
Dublin, Wexford, Kilkenny and Cork
**A Journey throughout Ireland, During the Spring, Summer and Autumn of
1834, Vol. 2, Part 2,**
Kerry, Clare, The Shannon and Limerick and Athlone

Aghaidh Achadh Mór, The Face of Aghamore — edited by Joe Byrne. This is a
reproduction of a title originally published in 1991 and is of enduring interest to
local historians and to those with ancestral roots in East Mayo. It covers such
topics as Stone Age archaeology, family history, local hedge schools, O'Carolan's
connection with the parish, the Civil War and townland surveys.

Lough Corrib, Its Shores and Islands: with Notices of Lough Mask - by
William R. Wilde, first published in 1867. In the words of the author: 'A work
intended to … rescue from oblivion, or preserve from desecration, some of the
historic monuments of the country'.

Lough Corrib, Its Shores and Islands: with Notices of Lough Mask - by
William R. Wilde, first published in 1867. In the words of the author: 'A work
intended to … rescue from oblivion, or preserve from desecration, some of the
historic monuments of the country'.

Ballads and Songs
Songs of the Glens of Antrim, Moiré O'Neill
These Songs of the Glens of Antrim were written by a Glenswoman in the dialect
of the Glens, and chiefly for the pleasure of other Glens-people.

Clachan
Publishing
Clachan Publishing, Ballycastle, County Antrim.